Pacific Time on Target

Pacific Time on Target

Memoirs of a Marine Artillery Officer, 1943–1945

Christopher S. Donner

Edited by Jack H. McCall Jr.

The Kent State University Press Kent, Ohio

© 2012 by The Kent State University Press, Kent, Ohio 44242
All rights reserved
ISBN 978-1-60635-120-8
Manufactured in the United States of America

All maps are provided courtesy of Erin Greb, Erin Greb Cartography.

Cataloging information for this title is available at the Library of Congress.

16 15 14 13 12   5 4 3 2 1

To Christopher S. Donner and his fellow survivors of the Pacific Theater of Operations of the Second World War, particularly the officers and men of the Ninth Defense Battalion and the Eleventh Marines, First Marine Division, U.S. Marine Corps—who left home as young men and came home as greatly changed men—and to their families and descendants, this book is respectfully dedicated.

Definition of "time on target": A method of coordinating the fires of individual batteries of field artillery to ensure that every projectile fired—no matter the location of the gun firing it—will reach the target area nearly simultaneously.

One's pulse beat faster and the appetite waned as the morning approached for the next job. Experience is a forceful teacher, and at no time at the front had I failed to see numbers of men killed quite near me.
   —*Christopher S. Donner*

War is sweet to those who have never experienced it, but the experienced man trembles greatly in his heart at its approach.
   —*Pindar*

Contents

A Brief Reader's Aid as to Unit Types and Designations

Jack H. McCall Jr.

In the U.S. Army and Marine Corps, the smallest self-contained combat unit is the company (approximately 150 to 200 men, depending on the precise branch of service and tables of organization), which is known in artillery units as a battery (and in cavalry and armored units as a troop) and which is typically commanded by a captain. Companies and batteries are further divided into platoons (approximately 50 men), which are led by lieutenants, and platoons are then divided into squads (8 to 10 men; in the case of Marine rifle squads, 13 men). The next unit above the company/battery is the battalion of several hundred or more men, usually commanded by a lieutenant colonel and comprising multiple companies. As integral parts of a battalion, batteries and companies are typically identified by alphabetic designations (A Battery, E Company, etc.). The Ninth Defense Battalion, for instance, had nine line batteries, A through I, plus—for the headquarters element of each of its three groups (Seacoast, 90 mm, and Special Weapons) and for the battalion's headquarters—Headquarters and Service (H&S) batteries. With more than one thousand men assigned or attached, the Ninth was an exceptionally large marine battalion. The Third Battalion of the Eleventh Marines had three line batteries plus one H&S battery.

The parent unit above the battalion level during the Second World War was typically the regiment, often commanded by a colonel. Unlike Army regiments, which specified the principal branch of service of the troops comprising it along with the regimental number (e.g., 223d Infantry Regiment, Sixth Field Artillery Regiment, 505th Parachute Infantry Regiment, etc.), Marine regiments were simply given a number, regardless of whether it was infantry or artillery, and the term "regiment" was not typically included when speaking of the particular regiment. Hence these regiments are called First Marines (an infantry regiment), Seventh Marines (also infantry), Eleventh Marines (field artillery), and so on. This historical quirk of marine unit designations may have partly originated from the long-standing creed of the Marine Corps that every marine is first and foremost a rifleman, and only then a specialist or branch-trained expert. With the growth of increasingly technical needs before and during World War II, however, more "specialist" marine units with branch-specific designations (such as the Defense and Antiaircraft battalions, Raider and Parachute regiments, and aviation units) eventually began to proliferate.

Regiments and battalions could be assembled into brigades (also often commanded by a colonel) or, more typically for both the Army and Marine Corps of this time frame, into divisions. The division was routinely commanded by a major or lieutenant general, who relied on the service of one or two brigadier generals as assistant division commanders. Divisions were further task-organized for specific campaigns or operations into corps (the highest unit of field organization in the wartime Marine Corps; for instance, I Marine Amphibious Corps or III Amphibious Corps) led by major or lieutenant generals, and then corps into armies of two or more corps, usually under the leadership of a lieutenant general or general. There were a host of other higher headquarters in the Pacific—COM-SOPAC (Commander, South Pacific Area) and CINCPAC (Commander in Chief, Pacific Ocean Areas) among others—but these were typically far removed from the worm's-eye view of Chris Donner and his peers and will seldom be encountered in this book.

Acknowledgments

Jack H. McCall Jr.

First and foremost, my most profound thanks are due to the man who wrote these memoirs, Christopher S. Donner: first, for having taken the time and the emotional energy necessary, not that very long after war's end, to record his experiences for posterity, and second, after many years of holding his memoirs purely for the use of his family and friends (with the exception of one copy provided to the Marine Corps' historical division) to make this exceptional manuscript available for publication. I trust that this book will do justice to his desire to let his experiences of war serve for the benefit of future generations. An equally deep measure of thanks is also due to another member of this remarkable family, the man once called "Toph" by his father, Dr. Christopher S. Donner III, who graciously and immensely helped by communicating with his father on family visits, reviewing the manuscript as it developed, sharing photographs from the family's collection, and providing both his family's history and enormous insights into his father's prewar and postwar experiences. While the memoirs were very well written in their own right, the introduction and context would have been sadly lacking without the input and feedback of Dr. Donner. To both Christopher Donners, father and son, I express my boundless appreciation and gratitude.

I must also recognize a debt of gratitude to several other marine veterans of the Ninth Defense Battalion whom I have gotten to know over the years, whose own stories parallel much of Chris Donner's wartime experiences. At the top of the list are Donner's "Able" Battery commander, Col. (Ret.) Henry H. Reichner Jr., and one of his subordinates (and one of the men who served on the grim burial detail of July 2, 1943), Joseph Pratl.

Longtime chair and secretary-treasurer of the Ninth Defense and AAA Battalion Association, David Slater, performed yeoman service in helping to organize newsletters and annual reunions, including the "Fightin' Ninth's" reunion in Chattanooga, Tennessee, in fall 1999, at which I first met Major Donner in person.

I also owe inestimable thanks to Professor Kurt Piehler of the University of Tennessee Department of History and Scot Danforth of the UT Press for reviewing the original manuscript, seconding my own estimation of its potential value to history, and making suggestions that ultimately led to my contacting the Kent State University Press; to Joyce Harrison, Mary Young, and the staff of the Kent State University Press for all of their assistance and enthusiasm in helping bring this work to a broader audience; to Kent State's readers, Professor Emeritus John Hubbell (himself a 1950s-vintage member of Donner's Eleventh Marines) and Steven Weingartner, from whose feedback and critiques this work benefited immeasurably; to Gina McNeely of Gina McNeely Picture Research for her exceptional skill and keen insights in combing the photographic records of NARA and the U.S. Marine Corps' archives at Quantico, Virginia, for just the right photos to better illustrate this work; and to Erin Greb of Erin Greb Cartography for her superb assistance in preparing the maps that appear in this book.

Last but not least, my love and thanks go to my wife, Jennifer Ashley-McCall, and my daughter, Margaret McCall, for their patience and good humor in giving up hours of family time and humoring me in my late-night and weekend quests as I hunched over maps, texts, photos, and the family computer in an effort to do full justice to the life and times of Chris Donner and his peers; to my mother, Patricia H. McCall, and my sister, Holly McCall; and to one of Major Donner's peers and onetime subordinates, my late father and another veteran of the Ninth Defense Battalion, Jack H. McCall Sr. (former Corporal, 1922–97).

Introduction

Jack H. McCall Jr.

> It's easy to see why men remember their wars. For most men who
> fight, war is their only contact with the world of great doings. Other
> men govern, sign treaties, invent machines, cure diseases, alter
> lives. But for ordinary men—the men who fight our wars—there
> will probably be only that one time when their lives intersect with
> history, one opportunity to act in great events. Not to alter those
> events—no single soldier affects a war, or even a battle—but simply
> to be there, in history.
> —Samuel Hynes, *The Soldier's Tale: Bearing Witness to Modern War*

It takes a special man who, having married the girl of his dreams after
graduating from Princeton and having just become a new father only
a matter of days after the Pearl Harbor attack, decides to volunteer for
the rigors of Marine officers' training and subsequent combat duty. It is
a truly lucky man who experiences and survives, largely unscathed, a
series of campaigns in the Second World War's Pacific theater. From the
lush, tropical island paradise–turned–killing fields of the South Pacific
to the shell-blasted ridges and villages of Okinawa, Christopher S. Donner experienced the life of both a Marine heavy artillery officer and, as
a forward-observer team leader, a "grunt" infantryman. Along the way,
he survived Japanese air raids and artillery bombardments, and he was
a witness to offshore naval duels (and adjacent to the accidental sinking
of a U.S. naval task force's flagship), the excitement of amphibious landings, brutal infantry fighting, and the agonies of numerous "friendly fire"
incidents. Ultimately, as a veteran of the legendary First Marine Division,
the "Old Breed," he eventually set aside some time in 1946 to write for

himself and his family a concise saga of exactly what he had witnessed and somehow survived.

One of the things that makes Chris Donner's memoirs so remarkable is that he actually survived three Pacific campaigns—the Central Solomons, Guam, and Okinawa—to tell them at all. Few published accounts exist of the experiences of Marine artillerymen in World War II; even fewer accounts can be found of those who served in the little-known Marine defense battalions. Further, there are virtually no substantial memoirs from Army or Marine Corps veterans who served as members of forward observer—"FO"—teams during the Second World War. The simplest reason for this dearth may be the nasty, brutish, and short life spans of FOs "on the line." The essential duty of FO teams is to accompany the infantry on the front line and get close enough to the enemy to be able to pinpoint targets and then direct artillery and mortar fire onto those targets via a near-constant stream of radio or telephone communications. This required a high degree of accuracy, with limited time and often a minimal number of test shots ("adjustments") to pinpoint the range to target. This also often required FOs to get within mere yards of their intended targets. The lifespan of an FO in heavy combat was notoriously short—often described as being measurable within minutes or hours at best. Given the violent fighting that Donner's FO team faced on Okinawa's front lines, and the casualties all around him that he so painfully describes in these memoirs, we can only be grateful, and somewhat amazed, that he lived to recount his experience of war.

Born on November 25, 1912, Christopher S. Donner Jr.'s childhood was spent in West Philadelphia, and he grew up near the campus of the University of Pennsylvania. Christopher Donner Sr. was a manager at the Franklin Sugar Company plant (and, foreshadowing his later military experience, Chris had several uncles who owned property in Beaufort, South Carolina, very near Parris Island, which later became the home of the Marine Corps' eastern recruiting depot). Chris's father died while he was very young, leaving behind his widow, Pauline, and their only child, Chris. His mother eventually remarried actor George Schiller, and Chris's childhood in Philadelphia was interspersed with trips to the theater and to visit a cousin who lived near Atlantic City and the famed boardwalk. As a high school student, he attended the Haverford School, a private country day school in Haverford, Pennsylvania. Upon his graduation from Haverford in 1931, he was awarded a full scholarship to Princeton University. He attended college during the middle of the Great Depression, and his mother took in laundry to give him spending money. Chris ran track at Princeton University, and once when running to a class he rounded a building and knocked Princeton's new star faculty member, Professor Albert Einstein, flat on his back. During summer breaks, he worked at the same sugar refinery in Philadelphia that his father had managed.

After Donner's graduation from Princeton, he planned to embark on a career in academics and teaching and, as he considered his options, did some private tutoring and worked for a Catholic parish. His engagement and marriage in 1937 to Madge Haas, the daughter of an Army colonel who was a former colleague of Gen. John J. Pershing in the First World War, was featured in the *New York Times*' society pages.[1] By all accounts, this was a very strong and nurturing marriage, lasting until her untimely death in 1983. Donner began his teaching career in September 1937 at the Chestnut Hill Academy, a boy's day school, in the same suburban Philadelphia private school league as his alma mater, Haverford. He taught at Chestnut Hill for two years, and then, in the fall of 1939, drove cross-country with his wife to begin his Ph.D. candidacy at Stanford. In the fall of 1941, Madge was pregnant, so rather than return to Stanford, the couple stayed in the Philadelphia area so that Madge would be near her family when she delivered their child. Twenty days after Pearl Harbor, the Donners' only child was born, a son, Christopher III, whom Chris affectionately calls "Toph" in his memoirs.

As a married man supporting a wife and child and approaching the age of thirty, Donner was likely eligible for a Selective Service draft deferment or exemption from active-duty service. But like many other men of his age group—including one of the Marines' Medal of Honor winners on Tarawa, Lt. Alexander (Sandy) Bonnyman—Donner responded to the call to arms, regardless of whether he would have been compelled to serve. Of men like this so much of the wartime officer ranks of the Marine Corps was made. The influences of his father-in-law and brother-in-law, both of whom were entering active-duty service, played a role as well.[2] In spring 1942, Donner began his training at the Marines' Officers Candidate School (OC) at Quantico, Virginia.

After completing OC and his subsequent officers' courses, Donner was assigned in spring 1943 to the Ninth Defense Battalion, then serving as part of the I Marine Amphibious Corps on Guadalcanal. The "Fightin' Ninth" had recently completed its first combat service on that blood-soaked island, albeit largely in a coast defense and antiaircraft (AA) role. A type of Marine Corps unit that only existed between 1938 and 1944, defense battalions were originally intended to secure and defend advanced naval bases and fleet fueling stations such as Wake and Midway Islands. Accordingly, these were exceptionally large battalions (some fielded more than one thousand Marines) and were equipped with a wide variety of weapons, light and heavy antiaircraft guns and coast-defense artillery predominating. Several of these units—the Ninth included—were equipped with sizable light tank detachments, and the first radar sets in the Marine Corps were provided to support their AA mission alongside gigantic searchlights and sound detection equipment.[3] As the tempo of Allied operations in the Pacific shifted from purely defensive to offensive actions, the Fleet Marine Force–Pacific began reorienting the seacoast defense elements of these battalions to serve as a heavy field artillery force. Donner's recent training at Base Defense Officers' Course landed him a place in the Ninth Defense's Seacoast Group.

Donner's first combat service occurred in the New Georgia island group. Located some 150 miles west-northwest of Guadalcanal, New Georgia, held a prominent position in Japan's post-Guadalcanal perimeter in the Central Solomon Islands, principally because of a large airfield located at Munda Point on that island. With its Seacoast Group equipped with eight massive, brand-new 155 mm M1 "Long Tom" long-range guns—the first of their kind to see service in the Pacific—the Ninth was scheduled to land on Rendova, an island less than ten miles south of Munda. The Seacoast Group was initially tasked not to serve as seacoast defense but as heavy field artillery, to wreak havoc on the Munda Point aerodrome and its surroundings and interdict Japanese reinforcements. As a newly assigned officer to A Battery of the Seacoast Group, Donner recalls having been proudly informed of this mission by his battalion commander, Lt. Col. William Scheyer. Of this prime artillery mission, so critical to the overall success of the New Georgia operations, Donner asks, "What could be sweeter?"

There would be precious little that would be sweet about this assignment, and the Ninth's deployment to Rendova was fraught with hazards. On the first night out, one of Donner's men was lost at sea, falling off the deck of A Battery's landing ship under somewhat mysterious circumstances. The New Georgia Occupation Force's command vessel, the USS *McCawley*, was accidentally sunk by U.S. patrol torpedo (PT) boats (although this snafu was widely attributed to a Japanese torpedo), and a Ninth Defense sergeant also became a "friendly fire" death while prowling between the lines at night on Rendova. Days later, on July 2, 1943, an unexpected Japanese air raid wreaked havoc on the Rendova beachhead in general, and A Battery's positions in particular near the aptly named "Suicide Point," mere moments after the battery had begun registration fires on Munda Point under the cameras of a newsreel crew and "rubbernecking" Army officers. Donner recounts the horror of the attack and its aftermath, when it fell upon him to lead a burial detail; the latter was so upsetting that he found it difficult to lead his men in reciting the Lord's Prayer. However, the Ninth got its revenge two days later on Independence Day 1943, when a battery of its 90 mm AA guns decimated a subsequent Japanese bombing raid with eighty-eight shells in only a matter of minutes. As Donner's account makes clear, Japanese air power was not yet finished by mid-1943. Despite the advantages of radar, a bevy of AA guns and nearby Allied fighter bases, the persistent threats of enemy air raids and "Washing Machine Charlie," a frequent nocturnal raider, bedeviled the Ninth and other U.S. units throughout the New Georgia campaign.

The New Georgia operation was intended to be part of the overall Operation Cartwheel offensive aimed at cutting off the Japanese air, naval, and logistics bastion of Rabaul on New Britain. This offensive had been expected to proceed relatively quickly. It rapidly bogged down, however, and ultimately required elements of three Army divisions and several Marine Raider battalions to secure Munda's environs and the small harbor of Bairoko by August. Once New Georgia had been largely seized, the Ninth's Long Toms were moved to Piru Plantation, and their barrels were turned toward the large adjacent island of Kolombangara. Donner recounts the bombardments fired on this volcanic redoubt, as well as the harassing counterbombardments by "Pistol Pete," a Japanese artillery piece that pestered the Ninth for days. He also describes vividly his and his fellow Marines' efforts to alleviate the tedium between combat. His descriptions of the fishes and marine life he encountered while swimming among the islands' reefs verge on the poetic and point toward what became one of his favorite postwar hobbies, scuba diving.

While the Long Toms and land- and carrier-based aircraft pummeled Kolombangara, U.S. forces successfully employed what became known as "island-hopping" tactics by leapfrogging Kolombangara to seize the next island up the Central Solomons chain, Vella Lavella. Now outflanked on both the east and west, Kolombangara's ten-thousand-odd Japanese defenders were withdrawn without a fight in late September and early October 1943.

With the collapse of Japanese resistance in the Central Solomons, the Ninth Defense resumed its coast-defense and AA roles around New Georgia. The Battalion was later rotated to the "R&R" base of Banika in the Russell Islands, from which it was dispatched in June 1944 to serve in the liberation and occupation of the American territory of Guam. Of this period, Donner summarily notes, "From November 1943 through December 1944, I was really rear echelon. Of the fighting on Guam, I can claim only patrol action." By late 1944, as the Allies' need for purely defensively oriented formations was waning, the defense battalions were converted into strictly AA units, and their non-antiaircraft components were redeployed or deactivated. Donner recounts the last days of the Ninth's 155 mm group and its departure from Guam to Hawaii. Although he had now amassed a substantial number of months overseas, Donner did not have enough time to entitle him to a home leave, so he spent a lonely Christmastime on Hawaii while awaiting his next posting, as he followed news of the Allies' travails in Europe during the Battle of the Bulge. His fond hopes of being able to remain on duty in Hawaii long enough to earn him enough points to be able to return stateside would not come to pass.

In *Wartime*, Paul Fussell notes the relentless transition during the course of World War II from "light duty" to progressively heavier duty, often accompanied by increasingly savage combat and destructiveness.[4] In Donner's case, this was absolutely true: his next combat duty would be with the famous First Marine Division, the "Old Breed," now slated to land on Okinawa. An integral part of the Japanese Home Islands' defensive shield, Okinawa's defenders had prepared a skillful and tenacious defense, relying on lines and fortifications laid well inland from the beaches likely to be invaded, in order to draw the invaders inland before crushing them in a *Tennozan*—a campaign intended as a decisive, all-out "battle for the Emperor." Although the Ninth Defense had certainly seen its share of violence and casualties during the New Georgia campaign, as it was a heavy artillery and antiaircraft artillery unit, technically, most of its men were not exposed to direct frontline infantry fighting. Donner's next combat service, however, was absolutely as frontline—and as heavy-duty—as one could be.

Despite his hopes of getting to rotate home from Hawaii, in January 1945, Donner was ordered back to Guadalcanal to be posted to the Eleventh Marines, the First Marine Division's organic field artillery regiment. After Donner's service for a time as a battery's "Exec" (i.e., Executive Officer or second-in-command), the Third Battalion's CO, Lt. Col. Thomas G. Roe—who apparently formed an almost immediate dislike of Donner—decreed that Donner would serve as a field artillery forward observation (FO) team leader to accompany a line infantry regiment, the Seventh Marines. In many infantry units, the combat life expectancy of the FO was only marginally longer than that of a company commander or first sergeant. The fact that Donner survived the hell of Okinawa— through weeks of combat duty in this capacity, no less—is testimony to his keen wits and survival skills, coupled with the presence of what can only be described as a considerable amount of providence.

On New Georgia, Donner had largely seen death from the vantage point of air raids such as the one that occurred on July 2, 1943, on Suicide Point. His saga of the Okinawa campaign, however, is riddled with death from multiple causes: from enemy artillery and mortars, from nearby snipers and machine guns, and even from friendly fire strikes. The terrain he often describes is blasted and seared; festooned with ridgelines, cliffs, and hillocks that provide ample defensive cover and observation points for the defenders; and often covered with decaying corpses. His team frequently sought shelter and observation posts (OPs) in caves and tombs. Donner's service in this infernal landscape took his FO team to Wana Ridge, the outskirts of Naha, the Dragon's Tooth, and Shuri Castle, to name a few pieces of blood-soaked Okinawan terrain. He also witnessed several incidents of unsoldierly conduct. In one instance, a stretcher team turned away from entering a ravine that was filled with casualties but under heavy Japanese fire until the curses and threats of their fellow troops motivated the stretcher-bearers to get going again. In another, an unarmed Marine jumped into Donner's foxhole; it was not until after the man turned and fled, barely responding to Donner's questions, that Donner realized the man was likely a deserter. Mere days before the death of U.S. Tenth Army commander Lt. Gen. Simon Bolivar Buckner Jr.—one of the two most senior U.S. officers to fall in combat in the Second World War and the highest-ranking American general to be killed by enemy fire—Donner observed Buckner and his staff near his forward position, virtually on the front lines. It was those very "lead-from-the-front" propensities that contributed to Buckner's death on June 18, 1945, a victim of shrapnel from Japanese artillery fire.

Although his humanity was assailed on all sides, he still occasionally found the time to consider and remain conscious of life apart from the war. Donner reminisces about listening to the then-current and enormously popular soundtrack for Rogers and Hammerstein's musical *Oklahoma!* while he was posted on Okinawa. He notes, in an ironic episode, one instance in which one of its most famous songs was informally performed on the morning of "A-Day," April 1, 1945: as landing craft and LVT (landing vehicle, tracked) amphtracks prepared to move out toward the invasion beaches, someone burst into a chorus of "Oh, What a Beautiful Morning!"

Donner unstintingly records the fury and barbarity of war in the Pacific, and he also unhesitatingly expresses contempt for the level of Japanese atrocities. His memoirs are relatively unique in that they report some instances of less-than-honorable incidents on the U.S. side as well, noting them at a time before most veterans were openly willing to recount incidents of misconduct and friendly fire accidents by Americans. The fratricidal losses on New Georgia have already been mentioned, and he recalls similar incidents that occurred on Okinawa. The extreme antipathy between the Americans and the Japanese enemy, commonly reviled in the frequent wartime epithets of "Jap" or "Nip"—as in so many other contemporary accounts, the reader is advised that these epithets will crop up frequently in Donner's memoirs—also substantially contributed to many aspects of the Pacific theater's level of savagery.[5] The presence on Okinawa of a considerable number of civilians added special risks and horrors, as the full extent of modern warfare between the Japanese and American combatants fell squarely on the island's civilian populace. Civilians fell prey to intentional misconduct by both sides, as well as to indirect artillery fire (to use that bureaucratic coinage of recent wars: "collateral losses").

Two incidents noted by Donner are strikingly illustrative of the horrors of war visited on Okinawa's civilians. First, near the town of Dakeshi, Donner's FO team was supporting an infantry company that was pinned down by fire from a small hill and nearby cliffs. As Donner began calling in his adjustments to direct the incoming artillery fire, he "heard the crack and spat of bullets hitting human flesh and felt the air move behind my neck. I instinctively flattened against the rampart as the bullets whistled down the road just a foot or so behind me. Two Marines within ten feet of my left shoulder had crumpled. The first bullets I heard were hitting them." After some ten minutes, a tank finally knocked out the Japanese machine gun that had caused the mayhem.

While the Marines were carrying the bodies of their dead downhill, Donner then "heard shouts of 'shoot the bitch, shoot the Jap woman.' On top of the cliff on the left appeared an Okinawan carrying in her arms what appeared to be a baby. She must have been allowed past our lines on that sector. There were shots. She fell. Then she struggled to her feet, moved over to pick up the baby. More shots. She went down and was still. When I could leave my post and go down behind the road," Donner concludes, "none of the men there would own up to having fired."

In another harrowing recollection, toward the end of the campaign, Donner found the body of a teenage girl not far from U.S. lines: "On the ground lay the body of a young Okinawan, a girl who had been fifteen or sixteen, and probably very pretty in body and face. She was nude, lying on her back with arms outstretched and knees drawn up, but spread apart. The poor girl had been shot through the left breast and had evidently been violently raped. With actual physical sickness upon me, I returned to the guns."

The experiences of war he faced on Okinawa undoubtedly troubled Donner enormously. Besides the deaths of civilians and destruction of their homes and villages, he all too frequently witnessed the killing and gruesome wounding of his fellow Marines and their Army comrades and the vile and fetid conditions of frequent rains, slimy mud, and the pervasive stink of rotting corpses that contributed to the special hell that was Okinawa. Donner bitterly recalls the loss of one of his wartime best friends, and he tersely chronicles the tensions of combat and of waiting to be sent back into combat: "The strain of repeated trips to the front was beginning to tell quite a bit on men and officers, although the officers caught it twice as often. One's pulse beat faster and the appetite waned as the morning approached for the next job. Experience is a forceful teacher, and at no time at the front had I failed to see numbers of men killed quite near me."

After being surrounded by such violence, hatred, death, and destruction, it is perhaps unsurprising that Donner opined afterward, "As I think of it now, I realize how little compassion we had even for the enemy dead. Combat had reduced our humanity pretty close to a matter of nationality." It may therefore cause little wonder—some 13,000 Americans died on Okinawa, not to mention 75,000 Japanese defenders, 10,000 Korean slave laborers, and 150,000 Okinawan civilians, and thousands of wounded[6]—that after hearing of the atom-bombing of

Hiroshima, Donner and his friends celebrated their enormous relief at learning of Japan's surrender as they sailed homeward for their first stateside leave in years before their anticipated redeployment in the invasion of Kyushu.[7]

Modern readers may find that Donner's reminiscences seem somewhat terse. Bear in mind, however, that Donner wrote his account largely for his own benefit as an *aide-mémoire* for the future. His writing style is crisp and detailed but may come across as rather controlled—even when describing those scenes that had to have summoned forth horror, fear, or revulsion at the time—and his relative lack of details regarding his wartime friendships and thoughts about Madge, his young son Toph, and the rest of his family may seem strange. This may be simply because he was striving to achieve a detailed but reporter-like "just the facts" effect, letting the stories speak for themselves. As a Marine officer and a gentleman, he was of an age and training when a man was expected to control his emotions. It is equally possible that having witnessed some truly terrifying scenes, the act of writing itself may have provided some emotional closure, and he knew perfectly well what his emotions and feelings were at the time of the incidents.

On balance, Donner appears to have been generally much closer to the comrades he made during officers' training and his service with the Ninth Defense Battalion—the latter, a period lasting some twenty months and also a time with better R&R opportunities for relaxation and bonding— than in his assignment to the Eleventh Marines.[8] In his role as an FO team leader—the grueling nature of which was summarized earlier—he may have been perceived by his Eleventh Marines' peers, bluntly, as little more than cannon fodder. As has been observed, veterans in combat units that were once quite cohesive but which have taken heavy losses often view replacements coming from the "repple depple" (replacement depot) with a jaundiced eye—sometimes even as little more than "fresh meat."[9] By the late stages of the Pacific fighting—after the First Marine Division had seen so much brutal conflict—numerous accounts make it clear that the Old Breed's survivors, officers and enlisted alike, tended to be less likely to befriend a new arrival today who may well be a dead man tomorrow. And, of course, few were as likely to become dead men more quickly than forward observers. Accordingly, the highly peripatetic, short-term, and intense nature of Donner's experiences with his FO team on Okinawa led to fewer opportunities to make close friendships with the officers and men of the infantry units to which his team was attached.

One puzzling ellipsis that may strike the reader concerns Donner's intentional omission of a description of his experiences at OC. As Donner wrote,

> There would be no use in describing the process, which had begun the preceding August, of transforming a civilian into the outward semblance of a Marine officer. There was nothing at all remarkable about that period of uprooting and training as it applied to me. In common with many others, I obtained very little from it besides the conviction that actual combat could never be much worse. *And, in fact, it had proved more of a struggle for me to get through those first twenty weeks at Quantico than it was to keep going through any of the fighting I personally met.* [emphasis added]

After one has taken in the entire breadth and intensity of Donner's combat experiences, the preceding statement is bewildering. His comments on his officers' training may call to mind the *Bushido* motto, which his Japanese adversaries learned in their own military tutelage (albeit one more morbidly expressed than it would have been in the Marines' training): "Duty is heavier than a mountain, but death is lighter that a feather." One very personal reason behind Donner's remarks may have been because he was a father and several years older than the average officer trainee, being just over thirty years of age during his training. Hardly a devil-may-care type, and being some years older and more mature than most of his fellow candidates, Donner may have felt the weight of OC's regimen more than younger men basically fresh from college.

Another answer to this striking ellipsis lies in the fact that even in the most horrific combat environment, a strong sense of camaraderie and teamwork helped bind Marines together, both enlisted men and officers, in "getting the job done," and that helped sustain both the team at large and the individuals comprising the team. This was in no small measure due to the rigorous training process faced by all new hands to the Corps. Marine Corps initial training is a process focused on breaking and remolding each individual's character to create Marines who can follow orders and function as a solidly welded team. While this was, and is, still true of enlisted boot camp, the OC process was (and still is true at its modern equivalent), if anything, even more grueling. The Marine Corps, it must be recalled, was, and remains, the smallest of the United States' military services. Even in a war effort as massive as World War II—which led to the creation of six Marine divisions; Amphibious Corps headquarters units; numerous Marine air wings; a host of Fleet Marine Force support and logistics units; and highly specialized outfits such as the defense battalions, raider battalions, and parachute ("Paramarine") battalions—the leadership of the Marine Corps consistently determined that it could ill afford officer candidates who did not meet its exacting standards of professionalism. This remained true through the war, although—as is seldom remembered—the Marines accepted enlisted draftees beginning in 1944.

OC was not—and is not—for the weak of mind or infirm of body or character: its intent is to weed out those unfit to be officer-leaders of the Marine Corps. To assess future officers' strengths and shortcomings rigorously, this training program is even more relentlessly focused than the enlisted Marines "boot camp" in finding each candidate's shortcomings and testing the candidate to (or beyond) his breaking point. No doubt, the rigors of this training helped prepare and toughen men like Donner to some degree for what they would later encounter. While Donner's self-observations are a mix of gentle irony and humorous self-awareness of his own quirks and foibles, he obviously was tough enough to survive OC and the Pacific and to lead Marines in combat.

Also, despite—indeed, perhaps because of—the small size of the Marine Corps, its officers varied from the iconic level-headed professional (e.g., Gen. Alexander Archer Vandergrift) to the equally iconic but legendarily crusty (e.g., Col. Lewis "Chesty" Puller), and it also had its share of officers who would have been regarded purely as martinets and malcontents outside of the service. That "it takes all kinds to serve" resounds through Donner's memoirs in his descriptions of his superiors and peers. The former range from officers he clearly respected, such as A Battery's Hank Reichner and the Ninth's commander, Lt. Col. Bill Scheyer, to the Ninth's 155 mm group's Exec, Major Hiatt (who comes across as something of a hothead), and to Lieutenant Colonel Roe of the Eleventh Marines, who for reasons apparently never divined by Donner, formed an almost immediate dislike of the "salty veteran" Donner. One may discern that some of Donner's descriptions of several officers' personalities presage Joseph Heller's literary concoctions of Major Major, Generals Dreedle and Peckem, and Milo Minderbinder in *Catch-22*.

Donner is no less critical of some of his peers: witness his measured but evident disdain for one lieutenant who claimed malarial symptoms during the embarkation for New Georgia. Donner does not gloss over the humanity in all its forms, good or bad, of his senior officers and comrades. Hints of the traditional U.S. Army–Marine Corps rivalry crop up, although on at least one instance—when his FO team is, somewhat unusually, supporting an Army infantry company on Okinawa—he joins his temporary Army comrades in a laugh at the painful comeuppance inflicted on an overly "gung ho" Marine officer.

The contemporaneous nature of Donner's recording of his memoirs adds a special level of color and descriptive reporting to this account. Being written so close in time to the events depicted, there is a special poignancy and relatively little revisionism, which lends his recollections a certain "you are there" quality. Donner, in short, seems to tell it like it is. When he says, "I do not intend to embroider the facts or the presentation," it certainly rings true, and his recollections of the facts generally gibe with most of what was known at the time. (This extends to his awareness—his precise recounting of the details of the incident being only slightly askew—that the USS *McCawley*'s loss off New Georgia was, in fact, not due to a Japanese attack.) Donner's personal scruples and background seem to come into play in another respect: profanity and obscenities, so prevalent in modern social discourse and many contemporary memoirs, seldom appear in his memoirs. We know that such talk occurred—although Marine officers of the day (Chesty Puller, Holland M. Smith, and other notably "salty" Marine senior officers aside) were expected not to resort routinely to barracks-room language in addressing the enlisted ranks—but it seldom appears in Donner's work beyond an occasional oath or Donner's acknowledgment that "we cussed."

After the war, Donner resumed his academic endeavors. He returned to work at Chestnut Hill Academy, teaching everything from mathematics and Latin to history and social studies. He became the school's director of studies and continued to teach there until the mid-1960s when his declining hearing—due to his close proximity to heavy artillery and shellfire, one vestige of the Pacific War that continued to plague him—forced him to discontinue classroom teaching. Donner then began a private tutoring service that employed other teachers. He also maintained a twenty-acre farm, northwest of Philadelphia, which served as the family residence. Eventually he helped establish the Philadelphia School in downtown Philadelphia. The Donner family farm, Sycamore

Farm, which featured an old Pennsylvania-style bank barn, served as the school's rural campus. Several days a week, a busload of city kids would range over the fields and woods of the Donner farm as they pursued various nature and science projects.

Donner retained his interest in science and nature after war's end. He had an appreciation of the ocean, both above and below the surface. Donner owned a small powerboat, rather prone to mechanical failure, which he based in Atlantic City, and also a sailboat prone to becalming. The beauty of the underwater reefs and tropical fish he had encountered and hunted off New Georgia's islets and lagoons captured his imagination, and he also took up scuba diving as a longtime hobby; he returned to the Solomons in the 1960s to explore and enjoy some of those former vistas in a peacetime setting. He became an accomplished scuba diver, even as the sport was only beginning its rise in popularity.

As a major in the Marine Corps Reserves, Donner would occasionally take his son to the officers' mess at the nearby Willow Grove Naval Air Station. Donner also occasionally attended the reunions of his first battalion, the Ninth Defense, where he was always warmly welcomed by the surviving veterans of A Battery.[10]

Donner's marriage to his beloved Madge ended only with her death from cancer in November 1983. After Madge's death, the warm weather and water drew him from Pennsylvania to Miami. Before fully retiring, he returned to the classroom, teaching in the Social Studies Department at Miami Dade Community College. After his move to Miami, he married Mimi Howland, the sister of a girl whom he had known as a boy growing up in Philadelphia, and they lived in South Miami until her death from Parkinson's Disease. Although afflicted with many of the typical infirmities of his age as well as his long-standing hearing loss, at the time of this writing Chris Donner is ninety-nine years old and living quite independently in a small condominium located on a waterway in Florida. His son, a prominent Cape Cod veterinarian, jokingly says that his father is "living in his last foxhole."

Donner's ultimate reasons for writing his account so shortly after war's end are best stated in his own words from 1946: "I feel that some of the experiences and individuals I met were worthy of clearer remembrance than my own memory will furnish as the years go by. . . . [Please] bear in mind that I write to preserve for myself the reality of a recent period in my life." That Donner was an accomplished scholar adds depth to the quality of his writing. Given, too, Donner's service in the First Marine

Division, the reader may be tempted to draw comparisons (and to note the passing coincidence) between his company officer-level artillery-man's account and the well-known account of another member of the Old Breed who served as a Marine infantryman on Okinawa and who also went on to be a college professor and teacher, Eugene B. Sledge.[11]

The manuscript was originally typed by Donner as one unbroken document. For readability's sake, I have broken the original text into chapters. Head notes are also provided to aid in the reader's understanding, as are several appendices and a glossary of terms.

As for the memoir's provenance and the editor's role in this effort: I first became aware of the memoir's existence in 1998 while performing research on the Ninth Defense Battalion, in particular its Seacoast Group, in which my father had served. On several occasions before his death in 1997, my father had mentioned a certain Lieutenant Donner of A Battery, who was regarded by the unit's enlisted men as being a good and well-respected Marine officer. After being referred to the manuscript by several Ninth Defense veterans—including Donner's former A Battery commander, Col. (ret.) Henry H. Reichner Jr.—I read brief excerpts in the Battalion's semiofficial history written by another "son of the Ninth," Marine historian Maj. (ret.) Charles D. Melson.[12] I then contacted Donner, who graciously provided me with access to his original typewritten manuscript and maps for my use. He advised me that the late Brig. Gen. Edwin Simmons of the Marine Corps History and Museums Department had suggested to Donner that it was worthy of publication, but, for deeply personal reasons, Donner had chosen not to do so.

This aversion to publication may have stemmed from several reasons. One of these may have been a perception that doing so might not be deemed respectful both to those who had survived the war about whom he had made critical observations in the memoirs and to the families of others whose deaths he had witnessed and described in his account. He may also have viewed any for-profit publication of these intensely personal chronicles as a bit mercenary, a form of profiteering from the agonies of war and sufferings of others. Fundamentally, as Donner noted in 1946, he had written these memoirs solely for his personal use, to help jog his memory in a day when his recollections might be more distant. Although occasionally cited only in small excerpts in others' accounts,[13] the manuscript itself remained unpublished at Donner's behest. Then, in July 2008, I received a letter from Donner in reply to a recent letter of mine. "For several years," Donner wrote, "no one has asked to see a copy of my account of the Second World War." Donner then opined that "it should not make any difference" if he were to "give careful permission to good friends" for the manuscript to be released to the public, but he was adamant that he wished to receive no profits from its possible sale. His explanation for his change of heart after so many years was succinct and thoughtful: "It may be good for people of this age to think about."

To edit this work, then, is doubly a privilege: both to honor the kind and professorial man whom I have come to know since 1998 and also to pay homage to the memories and sacrifices of the generation comprising Chris Donner's peers. I trust that the reader will find this, as I did, to be a keenly described and perceptive, but unstinting, look at war in the Central and North Pacific, as seen through the eyes of an exceptionally insightful and talented young man. I invite the reader to examine and marvel at this account, which, while clear-eyed and controlled in its observations, often painfully recounts how Christopher S. Donner and so many others of his generation—whether fighting for the Allied or Japanese causes—left a good deal of their youth and naïveté behind on those bloody Pacific battlefields more than sixty-five years ago.

CHAPTER I

April to June 1943

From awaiting orders on New Caledonia to joining the
Ninth Defense Battalion on Guadalcanal

It was probably inevitable that I would have the urge to write the following account. To one who has had a habit of writing journals and diaries,
the military censorship of mail and prohibition of personal records was
repressive, even if fully justified.[1] Now that I am off active duty and have
some free hours, I want to write a sequential summary of my years overseas. I do not intend to embroider the facts or the presentation. But, I
feel that some of the experiences and individuals I met were worthy of
clearer remembrance than my own memory will furnish as the years go
by. If anyone is so intimately interested in me that he or she reads these
pages, please bear in mind that I write to preserve for myself the reality
of a recent period in my life.

The gangplank at San Diego on the 17th of April 1943 is a good beginning. When I walked up it about noon of that day, I was already wonder-
ing when I might again set foot on U.S. soil and was bearing inside of
me the void of being separated from Madge. There would be no use in
describing the process, which had begun the preceding August, of trans-
forming a civilian into the outward semblance of a Marine officer. There
was nothing at all remarkable about that period of uprooting and training as it applied to me. In common with many others, I obtained very
little from it besides the conviction that actual combat could never be
much worse. And, in fact, it had proved more of a struggle for me to get
through those first twenty weeks at Quantico than it was to keep going
through any of the fighting I personally met. There were times in OC
when I very much wanted to quit, when my conception of the responsi-
bilities an officer must shoulder seemed mountainous.

The long wait in column on their pier, under a Southern California sun, under transport pack and dressed in greens,[2] had put us in a sweat by the time we found our staterooms in the *Lurline*.[3] At that point, we began to meet with the usual wartime conditions aboard transports: very little space, stuffy heat, and limited fresh water. Six of us piled into our small room on "B" deck. I thought that was cramped, until we saw the men sleeping on five-tier bunks with scarcely room enough to move between them. Let's see: there was Carr, Davis and Davis (not related), Wilson, and another whose face I remember—all of us, second lieutenants of the Fourteenth Replacement Battalion. Carr had come through OC, ROC,[4] and Base Defense Weapons School with me. He was a very serious, precise chap who had been nicknamed "Headspace" while we were studying the .30 caliber machine gun.

All that first afternoon tied up at the pier, they were handing out duties. The CO of our Battalion had been made officer of the guard, and he chose Jim Dyer, who "polished the apple with him," to do all the work. Having already been appointed as a censor for my battery to work under Battalion censor Aadnessen, I was handed no other annoying details. A checkup on my platoon of men revealed that they had drawn staterooms near mine and were getting squared away. The good chow was started that night in the prewar elegance of the after-dining salon. Ice cream was served twice a day, and the menu was really excellent throughout the fourteen-day voyage. A lot of pictures of wives and sweethearts were brought out that first evening before we were even under way. I used a precautionary "Mother Sill"[5] and turned in early. We were at sea when I woke the next morning.

The Pacific groundswell was already at work. From the first day on, there were certain individuals who always missed their meals when the waters tossed a bit. Fortunately, I had the "Mother Sills," which I had also bought for the men in my platoon, and I never tossed at all. A routine was established, which included physical drill on deck, rifle inspections, and mad scrambles for abandon-ship drill. But, for the most part, we liked to lie in the sack and "shoot the breeze" about women, or gamble. One officer was the talk of the ship when he ran about $50 up to more than $900 in seven straight passes with the dice. I suppose we carried well over four thousand troops and six or seven hundred officers.

The only women onboard were four Navy nurses, whom Dyer met in his capacity as OD. He introduced them around, and some of the officers were going up on the moonlit boat deck with the ladies until the CO of troops put a stop to it. A show was staged in the enlisted mess about a week out, and one of the plumper nurses lent one chaplain a bra and some other underwear, in order that he might do a burlesque of a strip-tease. He had great difficulty keeping his grapefruit in the bra. At the end of the performance, the chaplain tried to express his gratitude to the nurse, but she fled up the companionway amid cheers.

The blackouts at night were so complete that one could stand on deck and yet feel very much alone. The *Lurline* moved swiftly across the waters, by itself, following a zigzag course to elude submarines. There appeared to be little danger, and no one felt particularly concerned. Once, a deck officer confided to me that we had altered our course because of reported subs, but that was the only threat.

The heat became stifling in the crowded staterooms and troop compartments as we approached the equator. Beefy individuals were constantly developing aggravated cases of heat rash. Only the paratroopers and a few enthusiasts continued their body conditioning with vigor. When we "crossed the line" at the equator, the CO would allow few of the customary rites of initiation[6] from "fear of incapacitating troops heading for combat." By now, there was the usual rash of petty thefts to add to the heat rash.

And we had a stowaway, a man who wanted to go overseas so badly with his former buddies that he had secured all the combat gear, moved in line down the pier, had his friends create a diversion to distract the officers checking the sailing roster, and walked up the gangplank. This Marine had even obtained a liberty pass from his other unit at Camp Elliott in order to allow himself time to pull off the feat. He gave himself up three days out, and the whole platoon offered to stand trial en masse for assisting him. The CO reassigned him to his old unit.

It was funny how carefully I read and censored the first letters that were handed in. I even held them to the light to check for invisible writing, and looked under the lining of the envelopes. I could see something scrawled under an airmail stamp on one letter and, taking pains to remove the stamp, found the innocent word "free." We were all eager beavers about that sort of thing at first.

In the middle of the second week, we steamed into the harbor of Tutuila in American Samoa. I had my first look at a Pacific tropical island. The tall palms and steep, verdure-covered hills were as beautiful as are the mountainous sections of Mexico, but the heat was uninviting and oppressive after the ocean breezes. We were especially interested in the natives who appeared along shore, and we were rather surprised to find that the figures in red skirts, riding bicycles, were really young men.

We tied up to the dockside in the quiet harbor. I was given a detail of twenty-five men to unload one of the forward holds. Thus, I had a chance to go ashore and observe some of the native gangs of bulky, slow-moving, brown-skinned fellows who were working the cargo nets expertly, but with the least expenditure of effort. They seemed happy and carefree, constantly joking and laughing at one another in the Polynesian tongue. Some of the women who appeared, always under parasols, were colorful and also inclined to portliness. An ambulance was brought up to the ship at one point, and into the vehicle were loaded the corpses of two men who had died of spinal meningitis during the voyage.

Rain squalls developed quickly in the midafternoon, and we were drenched as the unloading progressed. I had an opportunity, however, to talk to Kent Bush and Joe Drexler, who had left the States a week ahead of me. They said that they and Hollingsworth were awaiting transportation to British Samoa and Funafuti, our most recently captured outpost to the north of Samoa. When we left Tutuila the following morning, we had taken aboard additional troops who had been garrisoning Samoa. Hunt and Honeycutt, both ROC classmates of mine, were among the officers. It seemed evident by now that we were headed for New Caledonia and Australia or New Zealand, but where our orders would take us off, we did not know.

We disembarked five days later in the picturesque colonial harbor of Noumea, New Caledonia, which was crammed with warships, troopships, and freighters. We saw what we thought were the battleships *Washington* and *North Carolina* and a large aircraft carrier. Barges made of pontoons carried us ashore. We loaded into trucks and wound through the wildly colored town, dominated by a large Catholic church and the old French barracks.[7] We looked in amazement at the blacks with their hair bleached to a bright orange. Young, attractive French girls moved through the streets, and everywhere were small-statured Malayans, the women resembling little dolls. The road led out to the country, past the nickel works, and became a heavily rutted dirt trail. The rain had done its work when we pulled up to the Replacement Center at St. Louis. It was a great mud hole, lying near the ocean in a valley between two mountains. One of the first things we noticed there was the terrific stench of the latrines. That was May 2, 1943.

Within two weeks, at least 50 percent of us had the "trots." The wet weather had severely complicated the water and sanitation problems.

When the "heads" filled up, they were pumped out in old gasoline drums, which were then hauled away in a truck called the "Honey Wagon." That was not a popular detail. All hands were called out every day to work on roads, ditches, tent areas, movie areas, and a built-in shower for the shack of the CO. The permanent personnel of the camp used our men to construct their screened-in tents, giving us, as transient officers, old tents. They took the mess hall for themselves, along with the choice food and the beer supply. We transients had no rights, except to handle the work on the growing camp.

A few visits to town convinced men fresh from the States that good liberty did not exist. The French were almost hostile; the stores charged outrageous prices; wine was $15 a bottle, whisky, $20. Officers could, however, buy a good dinner at the Pacific Club and beer at the bar until 7:00 P.M. Hard liquor was scarce. We took some pleasure on sunny days in the beauty of the land outside the camp, the "rivers" with good swimming holes, and the villages of Melanesians. These natives were said to have slit the throats of white men who had tried to get into their women. Whether or not there was any truth in that, the blacks made a fortune on laundry and invested their money in as many American blankets as they could buy at $20 apiece on the black market. To cap the recreation program and make liberty worth the effort, before I left, the French had reopened one of their whorehouses, at $5 a crack. The truck that took me to the dock went about a block from the brothel, and in early afternoon there was already a line of soldiers, sailors, and Marines a hundred yards long, policed by MPs.

The serious side of this replacement camp was the distribution of men and officers to units in the field. I entered it as a platoon leader and censor. Before long, I was spending all day bringing all enlisted personnel of our battalion up to scratch in clothing and equipment. (A lot of men preferred to throw underwear away rather than wash it.) Later, I had command of three companies, while other officers of our group sat in their tents with nothing to do. Then came the offer of a temporary job as headquarters company commander for the camp, succeeding a Captain Wenban, who was heading for the Ninth Defense Battalion instead of going home as he thought he deserved after a few months on Guadalcanal. I mentioned that I wanted no such temporary job, and I did not get it.

By this time, a group of our officers had been sent over to the newly formed Fourth Base Depot for supply echelon work. Baker, Bo, and Callahan were three of them. Jim Dyer was pushed forward by the major for second-in-command of Admiral Halsey's Marine guard. Jim was suited for that spot, both by temperament and by virtue of his years of enlisted service as a "sea-going bellhop." By the end of a week, he was sporting a jeep and a $50 membership in a beautiful liquor mess at Quonset Village over the harbor: really, a man to be envied. Larry Bangarer had a yen for real fighting: he persuaded the authorities to overlook his base defense specialty and was accepted by the Third Raider Battalion. Zorthian went to the Eleventh Marines, Les Bateman to Second Division's Special Weapons, Joe Foulds to the Fourteenth Defense Battalion at Tulagi, and McJunkin to a barrage balloon outfit in Noumea. The last three were in the tent with me and did not leave until after I had gone, but they had gotten their assignments earlier than me.

Meanwhile, the big lists had come in, and I was working until late at night seeing contingents of men off to the ships. Most of my three companies were headed for the Ninth, Tenth, Eleventh, and Fourteenth Defense Battalions, all in the Solomons. We heard that the Tenth and Fourteenth were getting plenty of bombing at the Russell Islands and Tulagi, respectively. I said good-bye to most of the good men and NCOs, who seemed pretty close friends to me after the voyage from the States. I began to wonder if I would be allowed to settle comfortably in New Caledonia while they went into the danger area.

Buck went into Marine Guard Mail Service, and Charlie Beck, my battery CO in the Fourteenth Replacement, transferred to the Casual Camp to help the major there. At that point, other officers had been sent to us from the code room of First MAC[8] in Noumea. They were Sandager and Townsend. No sooner had they arrived than word was passed around that orders were in the office for almost all the remaining officers. When the runner brought my copy to the tent, my breath seemed to leave my body until I had a look. Those orders to our first permanent unit loomed pretty large. I was going to the Ninth Defense Battalion, Seacoast Artillery Group, at Guadalcanal.

A large group left almost immediately. Carr and Caldwell headed for the Tenth Defense; many others left for the Fourteenth Defense; and Townsend, Sandager, and Joe La Cesa, a mild, good boy who had come all the way from OC with me, shoved off for the Ninth. I was glad to know that Joe would be in the same outfit. The word was immediately passed that the Ninth had had a long stretch in the tropics and were due for a rest in New Zealand. What a lucky assignment: to see Guadalcanal and then the Anzacs.[9] Four weeks in New Caledonia, in any case, had rested me so that I weighed about 155, was tanned, and felt some confidence in my ability to handle troops.

Late in the afternoon on the 29th of May, I heaved my gear onto the deck of the USS *Talbot*. She had been one of the old four-stacker destroyers, the "Holy Rollers," now converted for troop-carrying with two stacks and boilers cut out. Second Lt. Charlie Kohn was the only other Marine onboard, and like me, he was headed for the Ninth Defense. We made our bunks in the wardroom and introduced ourselves to the Army and Navy personnel who were both crew and passengers. Only a short time after we hit the open sea outside Noumea harbor, mal de mer hit the Army Ordnance first lieutenant who had been placed in command of troops onboard. The skipper therefore handed me that assignment and asked me to organize the gun watches. We had a three-inch AA gun, with plenty of 20 mm and .50 caliber guns. This was considerably different from that luxury liner, the *Lurline,* and the old *Talbot* lived up to her name of being a roller. In those first two days and nights before I learned the ropes, she banged me up plenty against bulkheads and on the ladders. Since the job looked important to me, I spent a good deal of time, day and night, checking the crews at the guns. In the stormy weather we experienced there in the Coral Sea, the decks were pitch black, but it was better to be topside than in the terrific heat of the small wardroom.

The *Talbot* carried about 128 passengers, primarily male nurses for the Army and Signal Corps men for the Army and Navy. Few of them knew anything at all about weapons, but we worked up a training program in coordination with the ship's crew. The idea was that the passengers would stand watch until they spotted trouble and would then be relieved as quickly as possible by the regular gun crews. One blond, high-voiced kid among the Army nurses came up to me and announced he could not take the position that I had assigned to him. Then, he went on to state that he was a conscientious objector and would not handle guns. I was surprised to find one in that setup, but I asked him if he had normal vision. When the boy answered affirmatively, I told him he could continue on as a spotter, and someone would be sure to take the gun in case any trouble arose, if he did not want to do so.

We made the run to Guadalcanal in a little over four days, spending one day in a fast convoy with an escort carrier. The trip was uneventful. Kohn showed little disposition to help with the duties, and the Army lieutenant ate no solids nor stirred from his bunk during the entire trip. I enjoyed chatting a good part of the time with an Ensign Christie, who had been a schoolteacher in Chester, Pennsylvania. The executive officer of the ship was a good man, who conducted me throughout the *Talbot* and explained the whole works.

When we pulled in near shore at Koli Point, before the mountainous green mass that is Guadalcanal, Kohn and I mistakenly stayed onboard. The Ninth Defense was positioned right there, but no one on the ship realized it. We sailed on another ten miles, descended by net, and went ashore in a small boat at Lunga Point. There were scarred palm trees, a temporary dock structure with a beachmaster's tower, and a sea of mud covering the area. After using the phone to call the Ninth Defense through eight successive switchboards, we went over to a newly constructed and impressive hall woven of palm leaves. This proved to be the new naval officers' mess. I met Barry Beach and enjoyed a fair chow, finishing up with my first atabrine pill.[10] Just at nightfall, when the mosquitoes were becoming troublesome on the strip of sand where we still guarded our gear, a weapons carrier truck arrived to pick us up. We soon realized how far we had come out of our way, as the vehicle proceeded with dimmed-out lights over some of the bumpiest roads I had ever experienced.

The adjutant of the Ninth Defense Battalion, Major Meek, met us and sent us down by the shore where the Seacoast Group's units were encamped. In a strongbacked pyramidal tent, illuminated by a kerosene lantern, sat Lt. Col. Archie O'Neil, CO of the 155 mm Group. He received Kohn and me, told us that we might be assigned to his group by the CO of the Battalion, and sent us over to another tent to sleep with Captain Wenban, who had preceded us from Noumea.

Wenban was a big blond fellow from Wisconsin who appeared quiet and subdued, rather younger than his thirty-three years. We learned that after having had a supply job with the Eleventh Marines for some time through its service on the "Canal," he had expected to go home from New Caledonia. Instead, his orders were changed, in spite of having twenty months overseas. O'Neil was a slight, dapper individual with flat grey hair parted at the side, a small moustache, and a very yellow cast to his skin. I was surprised to hear he was but thirty-eight, with a very young and recent bride.

The following morning, we traveled to Battalion headquarters, where we met Lt. Col. William Scheyer. I liked the man as soon as he spoke. He told us that we, as artillerymen, were to have a great opportunity. There was soon to be a push against Munda Point, the major Japanese forward air base on New Georgia. We would set up our 155s on an island across the bay from Munda and hammer the airfield. What could be sweeter? We would be expected to show real leadership, as befitted Marine officers.

The colonel then said that Brig. Gen. Pedro Del Valle, chief of Marine Seacoast Artillery in the area, would be willing to see us. We were ushered into the presence of this imposing brigadier, who received the two green officers as cordially as if we had been members of his staff. Del Valle asked questions about the replacement camp in Noumea, and he was distressed when he heard that officers trained in specialties were being used for other jobs. He made some notes, wished us luck, and excused us.

Kohn was no sooner alone with me than he began to complain of the bad luck that had landed him in a "hot" outfit. He was damned if he wanted to see any combat so soon after joining an outfit. I was uneasy myself, but I tried to tell him that if we had a campaign behind us, we might find it easier to go home earlier. He only sulked.

From there on, I was a member of the Seacoast Group and became immersed in the details of a training program that ran from early morning until late at night. In a meeting of all officers, I met Capt. Henry Reichner and Capt. Walter "Waldo" Wells (known as the Bull), the commanders of A and B Batteries of the Ninth Defense, respectively. Reichner was from Philadelphia, so I decided to join A Battery when asked to choose. The executive officer of A Battery, Lt. George Teller, was moved to "Baker" Battery, and so I became the Exec of A Battery. We immediately received the new 155 mm MI rifles (Long Toms),[11] which no one else in the Pacific had seen before. It was taken for granted that I would know something about these new guns, having been introduced to one at Quantico. With the help of Platoon Sergeant Paxson and other NCOs, we learned how to put the guns into traveling position and into battery.

Field artillery training was handed to us in large doses, and I found myself on the exec's phone hour after hour. About this time, the USS *Dent* arrived at Guadalcanal, many days overdue, having dodged several bomb loads from Mitsubishis in broad daylight. Seven men had been wounded on this sister ship to the *Talbot*. First Lt. C. E. Townsend, of Piedmont, California, joined A Battery, became the Exec, and pushed me down to Range Officer. Lieutenant Sandager joined Baker Battery, and Joe La Cesa went over to one of the Ninth's Special Weapons Group's platoons, although I had been hoping he would come with us. But Townsend was a trained field artilleryman, and that was all to the good of our outfit.

I began surveying baselines, noticing the parrots, and trying to obtain relief from the sun with dips in the ocean, which was so hot, one sweated when one swam. The sand was a dull black and rimmed with many strands of barbed wire. We had turned our seacoast positions and old guns over to the Fourteenth Defense Battalion in order for us to train more intensely. Just before I had joined them, the men had been issued greens (winter service dress) for New Zealand liberty. These were recalled, much to the chagrin of this "salty" outfit. Malaria had reduced the original forces that had reached the Canal in December 1942 to a mere handful. Now, each battery was being built up with new replacements. Able Battery totaled 116 or so.

A week after my arrival, I was having dizzy headaches during the day and sweating spells every night. I lost all energy at times and my appetite began to waver when faced with the tinned meat and beans. That was the process of getting used to the heat and daily atabrine.

The Nips must have realized what we were preparing. There was beginning to be an unusual amount of shipping off the coast, anyway. Early one morning, I awakened to hear Reichner shouting, "Hit the deck!" and then the explosive crumps of six or eight bombs at what seemed a short distance. In trying to roll to the ground, I became entangled in the mosquito net and only succeeded in pulling the cot on top of me. Reichner was lying in a tractor rut, nude and covered with black mud that he had never expected to encounter. Thirty-eight mosquito nets were ripped apart that one night in the one battery. Next morning, we all dug foxholes in the soft jungle earth and, shortly after noon, we were warned by sirens of a "Condition Red." The Japs on that June 16 tried to put through over one hundred planes. Most of them were caught by our fighters at the northern end of the island. About thirty-five flew in over Henderson Field and then out over Tulagi. I went down to the beach and watched. One plane after another plummeted to earth, several leaving trails of fire and smoke. I couldn't tell whose they were, but I felt excited. We were depressed, however, when we saw two LSTs burning offshore. In twenty-four hours, I had faced a rather impersonal introduction to aerial warfare, even though the first bombs had landed 200 yards away in a field.

We had many Condition Reds in the next ten days but saw no planes. Each time the warning sounded, however, the guns were put into traveling position and hidden under the giant trees. The crews became so fast that seven minutes was considered slow displacement. There followed the sure signs of preparation for a push: better food, including fresh meat and potatoes and beer. Life insurance was checked. Individual gear was handed out. Then, we packed equipment. The last week of June, we loaded LSTs all day and night at Koli Point. Only blackouts interrupted the work. We had a chance to test-fire each gun with only a couple of rounds, but the drills had developed good gun crews.

The tents had been struck the day that Capt. Bill Box returned to the outfit from Noumea, where he had been in the hospital for jaundice.

He was a Seacoast man of high standing, so Reichner made him Range Officer, which left me virtually unassigned. We finished up our beer and liquor the last night ashore, helping Hank pack his belongings for the rear echelon. The piles of his *Philadelphia Inquirers* made a good bonfire.

I had seen Joe La Cesa on the beach in the morning, and he told me he was slated for the first landings with his 40 mm gun crew. I asked him if he was enthusiastic; his reply was, "Chris, I'm not at all anxious about getting any closer to the fighting. Never know when something might be waiting for you." But he was smiling. He left the beach shortly after that.

When we had our Seacoast Group all drawn up, Colonel Scheyer made a fiery speech about this being our great chance to create history.[12] It gave one a sense of importance and a certain tingle to hear that. There was even a feeling of destiny as we marched to the boats that carried us out to the LSTs. Able Battery would land a day ahead of Baker. Some of the 155 mm Group's headquarters, with the group's Exec, Major Hiatt, were ahead of Able. And one of our intelligence officers had just returned from several days on Rendova—the island across the bay from Munda—with the natives, beside the very camp of the Japs.

The night before we were scheduled to sail, Kohn went to his tent and hit the sack with what he claimed was an attack of malaria. He was turned in to the hospital with a fever of ninety-nine, almost normal, and held for observation.

As our LSTs fell into formation and headed for the Russell Islands under cover of darkness, Townsend and I retired early to our bunks. Both of us were overtired from the long hours of loading ship, as we usually pitched in and worked with the men.

We lay all next day in the harbor off the Russells' island of Banika. The wardroom was the scene of a council of war for our ten or eleven officers under Lt. Col. Edward Forney, who had been assigned by I MAC to the 155 mm Group as special field artillery advisor. (Colonel O'Neil had previously come to us from Machine Guns/Special Weapons Group and was at this time on another of the LSTs.) Each officer was given a detailed instruction for the landing, the object being to unload the mass of gear as quickly as possible and enable the ship to get off the beach by midafternoon. We discussed the possibilities of being fired upon by Jap seacoast guns at Munda when we would be led through the narrow channel of the reefs off Rendova. No one made particular mention of Jap air raids, having full confidence in the heavy air cover we had been promised by the Navy.

Word came in from the radio room that the first units of Army and Marines had just landed on New Georgia and Rendova against very light opposition. There were no details. We knew, of course, that the Army's Forty-third Division was supplying most of the infantry, aided by a flanking attack by two Marine Raider battalions, a Marine air wing, and our defense battalion. There was tremendous activity on the fighter strips that we could see in the Russells. Corsairs and SBDs were taking off or landing constantly.

I checked over the items in my pack, carbine, and blanket roll. My carbine was the only one in the Battalion and came in for considerable attention. When I had asked the supply officer for some rounds of ammo, he went all-out and had a case of one thousand rounds delivered just as I was about to leave. And I put it aboard.

CHAPTER 2

June 30, 1943, to December 27, 1944

With the Ninth Defense Battalion on Rendova,
New Georgia, and Guam; the deactivation of the
Ninth's 155 mm Group; Christmastime in Hawaii

It rained that night, June 30, 1943. I slept fitfully until near 2:00 A.M., when I dressed and reported to the bridge for watch. There was some excitement among the personnel topside. Ten minutes before my arrival, one of our Ninth Defense radar operators, a boy who had been in my replacement company, had jumped overboard. He was one of those sleeping on deck. The man next to him said that he had noted signs of a nightmare. Suddenly, the boy jumped up from his cot and fell on the wet deck. He rose again and vanished over the guard wire into the dark ocean. The skipper, who had been summoned to the bridge, figured that the unfortunate lad must have been caught by one of the screws, for on an LST, there is a propeller near each side of the blunt stern. We heard, too, rumors that one of our troopships had been lost to a torpedo. (It developed later that the USS *McCawley* had overstayed the deadline in the Rendova area and had been sunk in the darkness by our own torpedo planes.)[1]

Lieutenant Jacoby relieved me at 0400, and I went below for an early breakfast of steak and potatoes. As dawn greeted us, the weather cleared and we could distinguish the Munda shoreline on the starboard side and Rendova to port. Destroyers were ranging along the New Georgia coast. Squadrons of fighters circled overhead. In fact, everything appeared under control. Our LST, the second in line, moved through the narrow pass in the reef line, its deck crowded with vehicles, radars, and men. We headed for the narrow strip of sand in Rendova harbor, at which the lead ship had already pulled up almost under the leaves of the palms on the plantation.[2] There was scarcely room enough for the two ramp doors of the two LSTs to be let down, side by side. Two of our 155s were on each of the ships.

My job was to assist in directing the unloading. A series of mishaps, mechanical in nature, delayed us from the start. Two tractor batteries had quit, and the elevator from the LST's tank deck to topside jammed. We had just succeeded in working out a smooth operation when, about noon, a siren gave three long blasts. I was on shore at the moment, designating a spot to place materials. The enlisted men busily working in the hold fled from the ship at the sound of the alarm and sought cover in the plantation. The Jap planes did not get through our fighter protection, but it took twenty minutes or more to round up the men and bring them back to work on the ship. When I had seen them run, not knowing how close the danger might be, I had a panicky moment and flattened myself beside a fallen palm. During the next two raid warnings, we stayed on the ship where we were and tried to command the men to go on with their unloading. Some did, and some fled each time.

The bulk cargo toward the rear of the LST had been horribly stowed. Puddles of burlap bags, barbed wire, and iron pickets had broken and tangled with everything. But with all of us sweating and clawing at that pile until sundown, we managed to unload everything of first importance. The 155 mm ammo, at 95 pounds per round, and the 90 mm stuff were all manhandled. I left the LST as it pulled out from shore and tried to follow the coral road through the plantation, knowing that the battery should by now be emplaced a mile or so away. The road had been churned into a sea of mud, in which weapons carriers and tractors were sunk to their hoods. The men who had been unloading were to remain at the beach under command of a warrant officer. I was virtually alone until I arrived at one of our 90 mm AA batteries. There I found Captain Box, who said that we should spend the night there, as there was no one who knew the trail to Able Battery. I readily agreed, being dead tired. The battery's CO pulled a couple of cots from a radar van, and we made ourselves comfortable under the tall palms.

I awoke in the middle of the night to a barrage of machine-gun fire. The Army, forming a perimeter defense a hundred yards inland from us and facing the jungle, were blasting away at something, and single rifle bullets were coming our way. But what had awakened me was a torrential downpour, which by that time had soaked everything I was wearing. Some enlisted men had thrown up a pyramidal tent and called to Box and me to come in. There must have been ten of us under the canvas, which leaked like a sieve. We cussed the trigger-happy "doggies" and went back to sleep.

The next morning was bright and sunny. The day, July 2, was tragic.

Box and I were given a lift in a jeep for six hundred yards, where it sank in the mud over its hubcaps. I was almost up to my knees in the soft ooze and so encumbered with my carbine, pack, glasses, dispatch case, etc., that I left my sleeping bag in the care of the jeep driver. He promised to deliver it as soon as he was pulled from the mud. That was the last I ever saw of that useful article. We passed a Seabee encampment where all the pup tents were half underwater, crossed swollen streams, and arrived at the Able Battery position. Reichner and Townsend were putting the last gun into battery, and the communicators were hard at work running lines. A small clearing in the palm grove had been expanded into a large field of fire by the blasting of over one hundred trees. Running behind the guns was a drainage ditch, and on the other side of this, the men had dug shallow foxholes the night before, all of which had filled with water.

Reichner at once began to tell us of what had happened to Sergeant Cox, chief of the Number 2 gun section. He had always been a pusher, anxious to have the best crew, capable of doing things faster than anyone else. Sometimes, the men of his section had resented the high pressure. Cox was made sergeant of the guard the first night ashore. He was told to post two men on each gun, to give orders that challenging should be carried out but that no weapons were to be fired, to use bayonets or rifle butts for personal assault. Cox, according to all men posted, had told the sentries to fire if their challenge was not answered. Late that night, the two guards on Cox's own gun crew heard rustling and movement and saw a shadowy figure approach in the rain. The Army to the rear was firing as usual. They challenged. The figure did not answer; it started to run away. Both sentries fired. In the morning they found Cox, his face swollen to almost unrecognizable shape, a bullet having pierced his windpipe.

By now, the gun crews were unpacking powder and fuze. Two press photographers were setting up newsreel cameras. A small group of Army officers had gathered near the Number 4 gun, to give the opening of fire the atmosphere of a spectacle. A large number of Seabees were working on the point to the left front of the battery, establishing a better road on the hard coral surface of the point. FDC was in the jungle to our right rear, using a ninety-foot tree on a hilltop as an OP. The mission was sent down for base point registration on Kokengolo Hill overlooking Munda airfield. The first rounds from 155 Long Toms in the Pacific began to crack out of the muzzles.

Reichner began to worry about the slowness in bringing ammo up from the beach. He asked Box and me to return to the landing beach and see what we could do about pushing through truck or trailer loads. I put my equipment near the Number 2 gun and went along with Box, noticing that a small-sized foxhole had been finished near the Exec's post, just across the drainage ditch from the guns.

As Box and I made our way over the mud-sunk trail, we could count the rounds being fired from our battery. We passed one truckload of ammo driven by PFC Baron. At the beach, two more LSTs were adding a mass of gear to that already stacked among the palms. I found the WO in charge of our supplies, and he stated that he had done everything to get vehicles through, but we could help him move things faster. I spotted a truck standing idle, and I walked over to it. Just as I asked the driver if he could help in moving a load of ammo, a 40 mm gun began to set the air throbbing with its fire, and I heard the guns of a plane open up. In a second, there was an avalanche of staccato sounds from the automatic weapons onboard the LSTs. I caught sight of the truck driver, now out of the cab, diving into the ground; others followed, and I instinctively went along.

Now the earth began to vibrate with blasts. Above the sound of the firing came the high scream of planes diving, and bullets smacked into the palms over our heads. Others strafed the LSTs fifty yards from us. Eleven or twelve men were packed into that hole, and everyone was scared. Three or four minutes later, the fury of the firing had died away. We climbed out. Across the cove at the point in front of our battery position, all hell had broken loose. Explosions were constantly occurring, and great clouds of black smoke filled the sky. From then on, it was known as Hell's or Suicide Point, where the Seabees were caught without even foxholes, working on the level coral beach amid gasoline and ammo.

Box and I did not suspect the worst. We found a tractor and trailer, loaded the latter with ammo and food, and headed back for the battery riding the sides of the TD 18.[3] Halfway, we met Francisco, driving another "Cat." His face was a yellowed mask as he told us that the battery had been badly hit by the bombing. When we reached the position, Baron's truck was still burning brightly, the tops of palms were smoldering, and large craters spotted the immediate vicinity of the guns. Smoke and the smell of cordite and burnt powder hung over all. Another tractor and four other vehicles were shredded by fragments. On the trail in front of Number 3 gun was a demolished bulldozer. And, here and there, were silent figures sprawled against the bloody ground. At first, I saw none of the battery personnel, but Box called my attention to the hillside behind us, where I could see them digging foxholes. I picked my way among the dead to Number 2 gun and found my gear, flat on the deck, yet a bit the worse for bomb-fragment rips. I was warned that a large dud had entered between the trails of Number 1 gun, and I could see holes through the inch-thick steel of Number 2's trails.

I dug a long trench on the slope of the hill near Townsend. When that was completed, darkness had come. I ate the remains of a K ration, pegged out the shelter half over the hole, and crawled in. I spent most of the night bailing out the rain that rushed into the trench. By morning, I would have drowned if I had stretched out in that "shelter."

In wounded and dead on July 2, we had lost about 15 percent of the battery to that short raid of eighteen planes, which had come in while our fighter coverage was out of the skies.[4] Our 90 mm AA guns, mired in mud, were not yet ready for action, so that the twin-engined bombers circled undisturbedly and began unloading in pattern bombing over the battery and from there on to the Point. They had caught the Army spectators of our firing and the Seabees without foxholes. One of our boys was last seen running with a powder charge in his arms. No one ever found a trace of him, although it could be estimated where a large bomb carried him into the earth. Three other men from the gun crews were instantly killed while heading for cover behind the pieces. Reichner, Townsend, and Paxson crowded into a one-man hole, with bomb hits not more than six yards on either side of them.

I chose five men to help me bury the battery's dead. An impromptu cemetery had been started quickly behind an adjacent aid station. It was brutal work under a boiling hot tropical sun to chip into the coral. When we lifted the bodies, the clustering botflies bit us in mistake for the corpses. Two of the men who were helping me walked aside and vomited. They were burying good friends. I was unable to find a chaplain around the hospital, so I asked the burial group to kneel with me and each say his own prayers. I was too upset to even lead the Lord's Prayer aloud.

The Army collected its dead, and the Seabees removed the indiscriminate mass, without heads, of what had been three men riding a bulldozer. Down at the Point, the holocaust had taken a heavy toll of life and created a mess of burned supplies, wrecked small boats, and water-filled coral craters in which bodies floated to the surface for many days. (That night, our radio picked up a MacArthur news report that a Jap air raid on the Rendova beachhead had caused negligible damage.)

July 3 was a struggle for all units to bring ammo and food to their positions. The water supply was easier, as it was taken from the cold, clear mountain stream on our right flank. More Army infantrymen were constantly arriving, many carrying two full duffle bags each. I could never fathom why so much gear was allowed each individual on the initial phases of the New Georgia campaign. Down on Hell's Point, we found hymnals and baseball equipment that had been landed by the first forces to arrive. Our own troops appeared overburdened, fatigued under the terrific sun, and slow to move. Already, the exhaustion of three or four days of constant labor and rain-soaked nights were causing recurrences of malaria. We lost the services of fifteen men by this cause in the first week.

Word was passed down of a Jap task force preparing to strike the beachhead that night. Sometime after nightfall, during the heavy rain, we heard the thunder of what we believed to be big guns at sea, but no ships came in to bombard us.

We were again blasting Munda on July 4 under a bright sky when Condition Red was sounded, almost at noon; everyone headed for his own particular foxhole. More than a hundred Jap planes made the attack, or attacks, for more than an hour. But, this time, our fighters were waiting high about the clouds, and Capt. Bill Tracy had his AA battery of 90s primed for action. As I lay on my back in my muddy hole, looking up between the palms, I could see formations of planes racing in over Rendova, where we were crowded into a beachhead less than a mile long and 500 yards deep. My heart was pounding in my head and temples with each crack of the 90s and with the tom-tom rhythm of the 40s. The sound of general firing came in waves of crushing noise as the planes swooped overhead, died to sporadic fusillades, and then mounted again to terrific crescendo, punctuated by the earth-shuddering crump of heavy bombs near at hand. I caught sight of one formation from which the planes began to spin and plummet earthward as AA bursts blanketed the sky around them. One after another they fell, until only a few remained to disappear from view. It was not until later that we heard that Tracy's battery had scored a world record for AA fire by downing thirteen[5] of this wedge-shaped squadron of sixteen Japanese bombers, with a total expenditure of only eighty-eight rounds. Great performances like that and others by the Corsair pilots and automatic weapons saved the beachhead from disastrous damage. I had waited a long time to see a 4th of July celebration which could actually terrify by its fireworks. None of it, other than AA flak, had fallen on the battery. Our forces had shot down more than a hundred Jap planes.

After the raid, I discovered that a small bomb had landed on the edge of the 40 mm revetment at Hell's Point and that Joe La Cesa had been killed by concussion. Not a mark appeared on his body.

A grim melancholy gripped me, which I could not seem to throw off. In a narrow-minded way, I became bitter that I was not having more to do with the direct firing of the guns, which the colonel had ordered should be exec'd only by Townsend or Reichner. I had to look after the camp detail of sanitation, which then seemed unimportant. Later, I had plenty of work with providing a constant supply of ammo at the guns, for we began to fire long missions to support the landings of the Army below Munda. We proceeded to construct a galley to serve hot food, a communications dugout, and erected a couple of tents, one to serve as a CP. Our hot food proved a morale builder, even if it was only C rations of the old stew type.

On the night of July 5, the Navy intercepted the attempt of the Japs to reinforce at Kolombangara.[6] We watched the tracers zip through the darkness over Kula Gulf and saw the bright explosions as ships were hit. All we could do was hope that our forces were winning.

And now began the night activity that began to wear us down. The Japs began to harass the beachhead by small, intermittent air raids, six or seven throughout the night, which kept us jumping or rolling into foxholes because no one knew where the next load of bombs would drop in the darkness. Each time, the sky above the harbor would light up with fireworks as the unwelcome "bogies" and "Washing Machine Charlies"[7] were caught in the searchlight beams. We came in the next ten days to expect the first warning just after darkness had claimed the sky. The last cigarettes and pipes of the evening would go out, and we would crawl into our holes as we heard the unsynchronized drone of the Nip motors. Very few of these were shot down, for they had no definite bombing run to carry out. Whenever they felt like letting go, down came the stick. We became proficient at estimating the precise point at which the bombs landed. Almost everyone was reduced to sleeping below the deck level during that period, in order to get more than mere snatches of sleep. Box, Reichner, and I moved into a tent with the "hot" wire, or conference phone, which Hank or one of us talked over and listened to during all air raids. Lieutenant Bliss, an observer from the Eleventh Defense Battalion, was also with us. Reichner was the last to dig a hole, and he came into my long trench at every raid, with a tangle of wires.

This underground existence led to some intimate contact with rats and lizards. One large rodent had a balcony running along the side of the foxhole behind the poncho that I used as a liner. Above, in the palms, sailed the black shapes of large bats, some with two- and three-foot wing spreads and bodies as large as squirrels. The natives called them "flying foxes" and ate them.

No sooner had the dud bomb been removed from between the trails of Gun Number 1 than we had a premature burst on Number 4, which killed two soldiers far in front of the weapon and somehow drove the base of the fuze back past the gun revetment and deep into the side of one of the gun crew. It was caused by a bad fuze lot, but it called our attention to a flaw in the barrel created by bomb fragments of a former air raid. So, Number 4 was out of action.

As the food supply grew scarcer, the men went off and shot a steer, one of those which had been running madly about the first two days of the landings. That was about the 18th of July and on the same day, we received orders to displace forward to Tombusolo, a small—really small—island in Rendova harbor. There, we were to set up as seacoast defense.

By this time, it was evident that the Army attack toward Munda had stalled badly. We were amazed by the number of psycho cases being evacuated from the Army's 169th Regiment. They told wild tales, accompanied by fearful gestures, of Japs who came after them at night with long metal pincers to pull them out of their foxholes.[8] We knew, too, that the Marine Raider battalions over at Kula Gulf were being badly hacked up by overwhelming numbers of Japs because of the delay. Theirs was to have been a swift move to cut off the retreat from Munda, but the Forty-third Division couldn't force the Nips to retreat.

The Seabees helped us build a corduroy road over the worst spots of Hell's Point. Then, we moved the guns to an LCT at that devastated coral beach. We had just finished loading the last gun onboard when we received word of Condition Red: bogies reported at twenty miles. These long-range warnings frequently were passed during the day without a plane appearing overhead. I began to walk slowly back to the old position to gather my personal gear when I caught the unmistakable sound of dive bombers coming fast. I looked up ahead of me and saw five white shapes zooming down from the mountainside. They had come in on the other side of Rendova and sneaked over the top. I dropped flat on the coral, feeling very personal about this attack, and as the Nips flashed overhead not more than 200 feet up, I could see the pilots' heads and bombs just leaving the bellies of the planes. In a moment came a series of deafening explosions, and I figured our guns were sunk. But when I looked up, the LCT had not been hit, though the fantail of an LST a few hundred yards out in the harbor was afire. (A fine captain in the Navy Medical Corps was killed.)

The planes were circling overhead as I ran as fast as I could to our 20 mm emplacement. They did not come back close enough, however, for us to have a shot at them. Box and I proceeded to Tombusolo after that with enough men to unload the guns by tractor and run wires. This little palm-covered gem was ninety yards long by fifty yards wide, packed with land mines, canister ammo, 90 mm ammo, several hundred drums of aviation gas, but no water. We felt as happy as if we were sitting on a live time bomb, and to make the place more attractive as a target, we found that PT boats were anchored on three sides, close inshore.[9] We spent a lively first night there through five air raids. Two hundred yards across the water, a battery of 90s barked their thunder and flashes at the sky, and a plane fell in flames.

The following day saw the arrival of the greater part of the battery. We set up for seacoast housekeeping in defense of Munda harbor. On that small speck of palm-covered land, there was no question of dispersal of troops; we were simply jammed in. A three-foot hole drew seawater, so foxholes had to be shallow. I trusted to luck and slept on the deck the first few nights, afterward moving under a small tarpaulin with Townsend.

The very first night after our battery had evacuated the old position on Rendova, the Japs hit the spot with heavy bombs. We would have lost heavily in one bivouac, and next to where our galley stood was a thirty-foot crater. As it was, our neighbors, the Twenty-fourth Seabees, were hit hard in the same raid.

We never fired a round from Tombusolo in the four weeks we sat there. We just watched the Army and the Japs slowly slug it out for Munda as the Army's Thirty-seventh and the Twenty-fifth Divisions became involved in the fighting. Not a tree could be touched on our island, for that would have detracted from our concealment. Hence, we built revetments of sandbags for guns and plotting rooms. Colonel O'Neil said three sandbags thick would do, over the height of the guns. Then, when he saw those, he called for three more layers, but by then the beach had dwindled to hard coral.

Water was always a crucial consideration. We were supposedly supplied 150 gallons a day by amphibious tractor, but the damn vehicle broke down every other day and never made up the deficit. We caught all the rain we could from canvas leading to oil drums. Most of the bathing and laundry were done in the ocean.

We were somewhat forgotten on Tombusolo, as the center of activity moved away from Rendova. Leisure time cropped up. Here was my first introduction to the beauties of a coral shore and sea life. There were many tropical fish of brilliant hues and clams with open mouths of purple, orange, and green embedded in the coral rock. Townsend and I tried in vain to construct a wire fish trap, but a raft of oil drums enabled us to move out to deeper water where we caught delicious red snapper.

Our fishing was also aided on several occasions by the Japs. They made any number of daylight raids on the PTs off our shores. When the tide was right, dead fish, freshly killed, were washed up for us. There were some weird specimens. Unfortunately, they also killed a couple of PT boats on an August day, although most of the crews lived.[10] The dive-bombers almost always came over or around Rendova Mountain and dropped altitude quickly for their strikes at close quarters. We set up two water-cooled .50s and, after awhile, claimed two Nip seaplanes shot down by our Tech NCO, Sgt. Herschel Cooper. He was later given a field commission.

The night raids continued in all-clear weather. Townsend and I were then sleeping on cots. Usually, one of us would wake as the bogies approached, and when the increasing noise of the motors told him the planes were almost overhead, he woke the other, and we hopped into our single broad shelter of earth and sandbags. Sometimes I prayed as the Nip dove close and released his bombs; other times, I joined in Townsend's heathenish expressions. (All of us were still getting over those first days on Rendova.) Several times from Tombusolo, we watched the Japs come in over the harbor in large formations of bombers and escorting fighters. We had a radio set up on the same frequency as "fighter control," so we could get all the dope on the realistic positions of the enemy planes and our own, which usually had to fly up New Georgia from Segi. Then there would be hit-and-run dogfights all over the sky.

One morning, we were awakened by the sound of heavy gunfire. We looked off the north side of the island, where could be seen a line of seven beautiful destroyers steaming slowly up the Slot. But, oh, what a powerful lot of five-inch shells they were pumping into the last defenses of Munda. The tracers were all different colors in the early dawn. Then, as the "cans" came about and tore at full steam back toward the Russells, the deep strumming of many motors could be heard. Formation after formation of B-17s and B-24s swung around and raced in for bombing runs, strafing the ground from their belly turrets. A dense cloud of dust, smoke, and flame rose and obscured Munda.

Munda was taken two or three days after that spectacle, and except for a couple of alerts that the Tokyo Express was headed our way from the Shortland Islands, we rested. A number of the men had come down with recurrent malaria, and most of us had lost weight. But there were some replacements from the Fourteenth Defense Battalion, and we felt rather fit. Baker Battery under Captain Wells had been moved to Munda Point, Captain Box had gone to Headquarters, and I had taken over the Range Section.

About August 22, Major Hiatt gave us the word that we would be the first through the Diamond Narrows to set up on the shores of Hawthorn Sound and open the long-awaited campaign against Kolombangara, Jap stronghold of the middle Solomons. He asked me if I were willing to do aerial spotting. I told him I would. He never mentioned it again and later selected Sandager and Cooper.

Two days before our advance party reached Piru Plantation on Haw-thorn Sound, the Twenty-fifth Infantry Division had driven the last Nips across the narrows to Arundel. We landed almost unmolested from our LCT, a few shells from a Jap seacoast gun having landed near the beach where we pulled in. The most exciting attraction was the teeming under-sea life in the channel: large, small, and many-colored fish, all swarming in the crystal clear water. Some of the Army men, who had been supplied only by parachute, were using grenades and taking out twenty-pound fish.

A narrow, coral road, paralleling the Sound, wound through the ave-nues of stately coconut palms. Approximately one mile from our land-ing, toward Kula Gulf, behind a thirty-foot ridge of coral was the site the advance party had chosen for our battery. The road led by a tre-mendous tree of more than 120 feet in height, into the twisted roots of which had been set an Army forward message center, and then on past lovely growths of lime trees. Along this trail were quickly brought the Long Toms, to be shoved into position by the "Cats," put into battery, and registered upon Kolombangara. The unloading was effected by late afternoon, though much remained at the landing site because we had only a truck and three tractor-drawn trailers to move everything.

Major Powell, a former officer of the Ninth Defense, came along as observer. He saw plenty of firing. The three guns then in action regularly shot about 2,000 rounds of 95-pound shells in the first five days or so. By the end of that time, the ammo handlers on the guns had developed a peculiar gait, with arms held down and forward as if to grasp another shell. They lived in the pits without time to wash.

We had not hesitated to pitch pyramidal tents under the screen of tall palms. Why worry when we had to blow down so many trees in front of the guns? But the first night that Major Powell was with us, he let us know that the Japs were still in the war. The major didn't think that he would dig a foxhole beside the tent. I was contenting myself with a one-footer in depth. But, by next morning, he was three feet below the surface, and I was still working to make my hole one in which I could stand with only my head above surface. One or two Nip float planes made dive after dive over or near our position, evidently trying to locate these guns, the nearest to them at that time of any American artillery. Each time the noise of the motor roared in our ears, we ducked, and as he passed on, we dug a little deeper. Just before dawn, we saw the dark form of a plane at treetop level, directly overhead, and then caught the whine of the bombs. The earth and coral shuddered to the *crump, crump.* We peeked out. There were shouts from the ridge in front of the guns, where an Army outpost had been established to man a machine gun. I ran over with a corpsman and some others. Two soldiers, who had been sleeping outside their holes, had been hit badly. Another had run off wildly into the trees. We bandaged the two, groin and leg, and sent them by truck to the Army. One died on the way. That was the first night's welcome at Piru Plantation and the opening of the drive to take the Kolombangara stronghold.

I was busy for the next two weeks with the ammo detail, unloading shells and powder from small boats and getting it up to the position. The ruts in the road wore deeper and deeper and then filled with water. New trails were tried through the green-carpeted plantation. The new trails made more mud. The tractors moving about the gun pits created a morass that could be crossed only by footbridges. Fortunately, our galley was on higher, drier ground, about seventy-five yards behind the guns.

In addition to the planes, which never again hit us directly, a new character entered the lists, "old Pistol Pete." Pete was a Jap 4.7-inch naval piece hidden on Kolombangara. He began to annoy us at nights. First came a bong (musical note), then a whistle, and finally a thud (which rhymes with dud) or the explosion. He used to fire eight or ten shells in succession and then stay quiet for an hour, and we generally took cover about the time we saw the second one land, if it landed nearby. But Pete never hit anything except a "head" in the neighboring Army unit. About the second week, Pistol Pete must have figured out that we ate breakfast; fired four hours; ate lunch; fired five hours; and ate supper. So he began to fire at breakfast, lunch, and suppertime. Our gunners would leave our pieces trained on the settings that our FOs thought could come closest to him whenever they went for a meal. Then, when he opened up, everyone would put down their mess gear and dash seventy-five yards—the nearest thing to an artillery charge. First one to his gun pulled the lanyard. This usually scared old Pete into quietness. Time and again, we thought we had him when he would pass a night without firing. Every FO who adjusted for him from the OP, 110 feet up a tree on the southern shore of Kula Gulf, claimed Pistol Pete. We never hit him.[11]

A very nasty little war was going on across Hawthorn Sound for possession of Arundel. Jap planes whined over us nearly every night, trying to hit Munda Field. The Eleventh Defense Battalion moved a searchlight and a 90 mm AA battery up by us. They never seemed able to get into action, and our men booed loudly whenever the light switched off as a Jap plane approached. The Range Section had set up the twin 20 mm and the .50 cals., which they wanted to fire. But unless the light stayed on the target, there wasn't a chance. The men could not understand that the Eleventh Defense was acting under orders. I still don't understand what their orders were.

By the beginning of October, the Seabees were constructing a fighter strip for New Zealand P-40s down by our landing. I had made a two-day trip to Munda, where I was told of my promotion to first lieutenant and passed a physical in which I had to say "Ah," and that was about all. Munda was being done over in a big way. There were hundreds of planes. We had located a Solomon Islands dugout canoe by this time. Private Fotormy, Sperling, and I did some fishing—with dynamite. We caught enough for the battery. This and heart of palm were our only fresh fare. In fact, food was becoming scarce. The men did manage to run down a plantation cow from which everyone had a small slice of "outlaw" meat, but the diet of beans and C-ration hash was hard to take for weeks on end. I tried swimming in Hawthorn Sound, and when I found some shells from Pistol Pete landing in the water nearby, I ducked for shore, scraping my leg on coral en route. The injury later became infected.

By October 3, the Army had knocked the Japs off Arundel. Preparations were being made for the push into Kolombangara itself. We all had visions of the Nips making a last-ditch defense from the jungled sides of the 6,000-foot peak above Vila airfield. Air raids on the fortress increased, and Army artillery helped us pour thousands of shells into the place. On one day, for certain visiting brass hats, we joined (B Battery had now taken a position next to us) five other battalions in massed fires. On October 8, the Army moved into Kolombangara. The Japs, it was discovered, had moved out the night before. The battle for the Central Solomons was over. We went over in patrols from the Ninth Defense to have a look at the damage we had helped to inflict. It was after a twelve-mile hike on the mountainside of Kolombangara in 125-degree heat that my leg injury became aggravated enough—my leg swelled, a fever and vomiting developed—to put me in the naval hospital at Munda for three days (October 11–14). We spent at least half of each night in the hospital air raid shelter, so I was really happy to get back to the battery.

The offensive role of the Long Toms was concluded with this engagement. We had fired our fool heads off as field artillery, and now we went into defensive position. There were still air raids, but by November 1, 1943, the action had shifted north to Bougainville and we were in a rear area, really acting as protection for the fighter and bomber groups around Munda. We could relax a little.

We live with personalities: we get along, and we clash. At the top of the Ninth had been Colonel Scheyer. But when he was moved upstairs, Archie "Blood and Guts" O'Neil (a slight, vacillating gentleman) took over. This move left Major "Turret-Top" Hiatt, a.k.a. the "Lobster," in command of our group, while Lieutenant Colonel Taylor, known to the older officers as "TORSOB" (The Original Revolving Son-of-a-Bitch), became Exec for the Battalion. Dissatisfaction began with this lineup of personalities, and matters were not helped at all by delays and even failure to forward ammo, supplies, and particularly food from headquarters at Munda. Being farthest away from the center of the Battalion (five miles by boat only), the 155s had pretty fair reasons for feeling disgruntled.

To make matters worse, our own group CO put his claws on everything he saw. If a battery succeeded in obtaining a little lumber or fresh chow for itself, the Lobster would commandeer this for his group headquarters. Of course, he went up to the OP and fired a lot, but the stories came back of targets such as a single Jap on a motorcycle, a group of them swimming, or of "creeping" by full volleys for four adjustments—all of which landed in water. Such stories are passed around when confidence is lacking. And I wasn't feeling too happy about being stuck on the ammo detail and not being allowed to "exec" the battery unless both Reichner and Townsend were away, which happened once when Reichner took a breather in Guadalcanal. I rather blamed the latter for not giving me more responsibility, although I must have appeared quite a character, sometimes writing poetry in my spare moments[12] and being ever alert for the heart of palm in newly chopped trees, or even perfecting my standing-type foxhole outside the tent.

There were little things to take our minds off ourselves once the action had cooled. Some explosive under the corpsman's bunk blew up one night while he was asleep and burned the tent around his ears without hurting him. Francisco, a powerful man, tried to disassemble a Jap fuze and was peppered by fragments when it went off, so that he almost lost sight in one eye. While Pistol Pete was still in action, a rubbish fire was started by day, which sprang up again by night. I took some men with shovels, and while we were covering it with dirt, rounds from Pete landed close enough to scare us plenty—and even then, the fire glowed again. Reichner went out himself to douse the embers and suffered another barrage from the Japs. He was fit to be tied when he returned.

About October 20, we were moved to a point at the end of Munda Field. In bulldozing for our mess hall, we dug up a number of Japs, whose stench never did leave the place. But here, we enjoyed our first seagoing "head" on which we could sit and watch the mullet swim by or a plane burst into flame overhead.

I caught a chest cold and visited the Battalion doctor for treatment. He figured that I was very low on weight, 137 pounds, and thought he detected a heart murmur. He recommended further observation in the naval hospital at Guadalcanal. The next day, I reported to MOB 8[13] for evacuation by air. One of those freak coincidences occurred. Naval Lieutenant (j.g.) Christie, who had come up from Noumea with me, was also slated for evacuation because of malaria. He had been through most of the New Georgia action. We flew the 140 miles next morning, and I had my first aerial view of the fascinatingly beautiful lagoons and islets of the New Georgia and Russell Islands. I spent ten days in the hospital in the surgical ward. The doctors gave me all sorts of tests and decided a good rest would fix up the heart, which did not appear especially bad. By that time, the Ninth had received the promise of thirty days' leave to New Zealand. The doctor offered to send me to Noumea, but, thinking that we would be headed to real liberty, I said I preferred to rejoin the outfit. I flew back weighing six pounds heavier from better food, but I never saw New Zealand.

The battery had moved to Nusalavata, as pretty a little island as ever existed, just 150 yards long and about 90 yards wide. In a seacoast position, virtually our own masters, we loafed and wanted only for food and drink. I shall never forget the placid, clear-blue beauty of the lagoon beside which we pitched our tents.

From November 1943 through December 1944, I was really rear echelon. Of the fighting on Guam, I can claim only patrol action.

We loved Nusalavata, where I once met the son of the chief who owned the island. In January 1944, we moved to Roviana for embarkation; then, we set up camp on Banika in the Russells, where we trained for the next push and had our first liquor in a long time, together with plenty of beer and a look at some Red Cross girls, nurses, and entertainers. I spent a few weeks at a field artillery school on Guadalcanal during May.

During June and July 1944, we loaded ship and on July 20th we boarded a Victory vessel. We—the 155 Group, that is, the AA portion of the Ninth having gone in on the initial push at Guam—stayed aboard that scow, manned by an abominable Merchant Marine crew, for just about a month, laying over a week at Eniwetok. We landed in Guam at about the time organized fighting was coming to an end. Yet even as we unloaded at the Piti Point naval base, sniper activity went on around the harbor. Guam was novel, and the people interesting to those of us who had been so long in the jungles and palm groves. But, we were busy building a position high above Adelup Point, running patrols across the island, and I spent many hours writing letters home to Madge. The latter tells most of that life.[14]

There is a special story that the letters to home did not tell about a short, pockmarked Californian. He had gone overseas with my replacement unit; had served with a machine-gun unit giving our battery protection at Piru Plantation; and on his application, had been transferred to A Battery's roster. He obtained a guitar from a Seabee, which he played for the appreciative audience we furnished on Nusalavata and Banika. This man obviously possessed a romantic soul to go with his Spanish lyrics. After we had established ourselves on Guam and were even granting liberties for visiting, he used to go forth frequently. When he overstayed a couple of liberties, Townsend, who had received command of the battery when Reichner became Group Exec, gave the man special duty and restriction. On the next liberty day, the Californian said he was sick, but our corpsman declared he could find nothing meriting removal of the man to the hospital. He thereupon gained access to Townsend and told the latter he was the cause of many nightmares. Townsend was astounded and ordered him out. He then claimed his right to see the chaplain and was sent up to Battalion headquarters. The "Padre" called us up later and said he was placing our man in sick bay, although he could not see anything wrong with him. That was at 5 P.M. At 8 P.M., the Padre phoned excitedly that our young Californian had disappeared from sick bay. At 9 P.M., the chaplain again phoned: "Townsend," he said indignantly, "I am putting your man on report. No one is going to hide behind the cloak of the Lord and get away with it, as far as I'm concerned." "Where was he found?" "In an enlisted men's head, having intercourse with a Guamanian girl!" (Rear echelon!)

The Ninth Defense Battalion had now become the Ninth AA Battalion and the Ninth Seacoast Group. New officers took over the AA, but Warrant Officers Ballinger and Kersh; Lieutenants Sandager, Beger, and Townsend; Captains Box, Teller, and Carr; and Majors Reichner, Wenban, and Waldo Wells are the ones I shall remember. The old-timers left one at a time for home, and we saw them off with rousing parties.

On the 7th of December 1944, the Ninth Seacoast Group boarded trucks in the area of the Ninth AA. The new CO of that unit came down to see us off under command of Major Wells. Only a few men raised their heads to watch us leave. There were no cheers, although a lot of buddies who had come a long way together were parting. We boarded ship at Sumy and were in Pearl Harbor by December 17. In Europe, the Battle of the Bulge was beginning. In the Replacement Center, U.S. Marines, outside Honolulu, the Ninth Seacoast Group was dissolved. Three-fifths of the personnel shipped back to the States; all those with twenty-two months overseas went home. A lot of us with twenty-one months overseas or less remained. That first night in Hawaii, when I heard that news, I drank more beer than I care to remember.

We took liberty in Honolulu. That meant seeing the town, standing at the crowded intersections downtown and smelling the civilized people as they passed; the gaily dressed women made me yearn to be home. We dropped in at the Marine Officers' Club for drinks and watched the officers regularly stationed in Hawaii dance with the attractive girls, while we discussed the scuttlebutt about the next moves toward Japan. We saw Townsend, Kersh, Ballinger, Teller, and Sandager off by plane in a blaze of champagne and glory. Most of the men left by ship, with Waldo Wells in command. And, on Christmas—after finding that I couldn't phone Madge, after piling up a good hangover at the club—I had the duty of censoring letters and equipping troops headed for Iwo Jima or the Solomons. Sure,

Hawaii was beautiful, but most of those whom I knew had gone home, and I had just about missed the boat. Beside that cause of melancholy, the Battle of the Bulge was only another of the Army's mistakes.

Twenty-one months in the tropics: that was long enough to take the edge off anyone's enthusiasm for another crack at the enemy. After Christmas, some of the enlisted men with the same time overseas were sent to local motor transport, where they might serve until twenty-two or twenty-three months would give them enough time for stateside liberty. Perhaps there was hope for a spot at the Replacement Center. Many of the officers in my own ROC had fine apartments and jeeps. Would they retain us and send others out?

On December 27, Toph's birthday, Bill Sigler and I were ordered to join the First Marine Division back in the Russell Islands.

CHAPTER 3

December 27, 1944, to
March 31, 1945

Reassignment from Hawaii to the Eleventh Marines,
First Marine Division; preparations for the invasion of Okinawa

I finally called Madge's friend, Mrs. Ben Dillingham, who, with her husband, entertained me at lunch in a lovely home near the University of Hawaii. I felt so awkward in a civilized house that I all but fell on my face, and I did spill a cocktail on the lounge. But I liked the Dillinghams, and I enjoyed myself immensely after two more cocktails had gone down the right direction.

On December 30, 1944, we climbed into a C-54 at the Navy's big field and took off about 9:00 A.M. It was cold weather at 10,000 feet, and we wrapped ourselves in blankets. There was a stop at Johnson Island for lunch, and by 8:30 P.M., having passed the International Date Line, we landed at Kwajalein. There, on a bench in the Quonset hut that was the air terminal for Johnson Island, I saw in the year 1945 through half-closed eyes. At 1:30 A.M., we climbed aboard again to reach Guadalcanal and its sweltering heat before 8:00 A.M. During the trip, we picked up some sleep while rolled in blankets on the floor of the plane. I met a young Captain Hennessey, a stocky, rosy-cheeked fellow who had been with the First Division during some of the fighting on Guadalcanal. He had served more than a year in the States and was now rejoining the First Division. Of course, there was plenty for me to ask him about life and conditions in the United States.

Those of us headed for the First took an APC from the Canal to the Russells. Sigler and I reported in at the Eleventh Marines, only to find that the outfit was training on the Canal, having left just a small headquarters detachment behind at Pavuvu. So, after being equipped, we took command of some First Marine Division infantrymen going aboard an LSM and sailed back past Koli Point to the Eleventh Marines' encampment.

It must have been on January 6, 1945, that we walked into Colonel "Big Foot" Brown's office, met his Exec, Colonel Lyman, and were assigned to the Third Battalion, Eleventh Marines, over the protest of Lieutenant Colonel Roe, who said he wanted no more ex-seacoast officers.

The Second and Third Battalions were camped next to one another, with the officers' tents along a single street in "officers' country" under some large trees. On arrival, I met Bud Honeycutt and Bayroor Zorthian, along with MacDonald, all from my ROC, and the welcome was friendly. Then I went in for an interview with Colonel Roe and his Exec, Major Wooster. They scarcely troubled to find out if I had ever seen combat of any sort but asked if I knew anything of QM work. I said my line had been Range Section, Survey, and Ammo. That rather disappointed Roe, but he assigned me to H Battery to understudy Dick Woods, the Exec; Captain MacBride, who was then CO; Lieutenant Gibson, range officer; Lt. John Williams; and Michevich, assigned to FO duty. I met my fellow battery officers, but I continued to sack in a tent with Honeycutt.

The routine was much more active than that to which I had been accustomed in the Ninth Defense during its periods of training. We rose early, spent most of the day in the field with gun drill or firing problems, had field artillery classes in the evening, and wound up with several hours at the bar. I limited my drinking but spent considerable time shooting the breeze and joining the wildly enthusiastic singing of "Waltzing Matilda," "I've Got Tuppence," "Call Out the Army and the Navy," etc. I was coming along rather well as a Battery Exec. Dick Woods was businesslike and helpful; Johnny Williams, amusing and friendly; Gibson, a trifle surly, on purpose; Michevich, fat, lazy, and unwilling to take responsibility. Perhaps I impressed them too much as an "eager beaver" type, for I busied myself in the work to make the days pass more quickly. MacBride was easygoing.

Sigler had been assigned to George Battery. Other new officers joined. An old-time Marine, Warrant Officer Franklin, took over Ordnance, and young Lieutenant Perkins joined "Item" Battery.[1] We were all together so that I had an excellent opportunity to meet all the officers of the Second and Third Battalions, especially big Lt. Col. Jim Moffatt of the Second, who could drink more than any man in the regiment and still do a better job next morning that anyone else. The First Sergeant of How Battery was a character, an old China Marine, who was not yet as old as I, but he seemed so. He had the men lined up, toeing the mark, but thinking him a first-class NCO, which he was. No man in the Battalion could give a newcomer more helpful advice.

The work went on normally for two weeks, and then came distinct changes. Capt. Bill Miller, Captain Brown, and one or two others who had been stateside for thirty-day leaves following Peleliu returned to the outfit. At once, the colonel kicked MacBride upstairs to serve as the Battalion's liaison with the infantry, gave How Battery to Miller, and shifted Michevich and me around so that I became an FO. The reason for the latter shift, said Roe, was that he refused to send Michevich to represent us with the infantry and that we must soon team up with the Seventh Marines. It meant, of course, that I must learn the roughest job in the Field Artillery, one in which I had had no experience. I knew, too, what it would imply for any future action.

John Williams was told to instruct me a bit, and while that helped, I could not find the heart for this new line after having just attained fair proficiency in the work at the battery. I felt that as second-ranking officer in the battery, I could have been worked into the Range Section if they did not want to keep me with the guns, for the FOs were usually only junior lieutenants. But I was to find that this was not Roe's idea of running a battery.

After a few initial problems with our own artillery, we worked for a while with the armored amphtracks,[2] "teaching" them in FA methods. Then the Seventh Marines moved down from Pavuvu, and Williams and I were sent over to live with them. We were teamed with the Second Battalion, under command of Colonel Berger. And there was Huff, another spindly Georgian from our ROC, now Battalion-2. I met, too, the three company commanders, Norton, Grass, and Beardsley, rugged, alert men and excellent troop leaders.

For a week, we went out on maneuvers at daybreak or in the middle of the night, laying wire and lugging "510"[3] radios through the jungles, plains, and rivers of Guadalcanal. I learned how to operate the sets and phones, send messages in code, and arrange barrages of a sort. Above all, I had an insight into how the infantry really moves in the jungle, how fouled up it can become in such movement, and how little one should carry along as personal gear. The maneuvers made the general plan of our next combat quite clear. Our Third Battalion would be in direct support of the Seventh Marines, with G, H, and I Batteries teaming with the First, Second, and Third Battalions, respectively, of the Seventh Marines.

It made the next push seem nearer, more personalized, and yet I felt no desire to pry around to learn where the strike would hit.

The Seventh was now loaded with a group of new, green lieutenants who had come out from the States. Young Mason was one, and there were two 1944 Annapolis grads, along with some others. These men were tried in all the different jobs but usually wound up as platoon leaders. I enjoyed looking up my old friend John Duplantis in First Battalion. He was now the Exec of a company, the only officer of that company who had survived Peleliu during the previous year. He seemed a lot more mature than when he used to raise hell in ROC. Cape Gloucester in 1943 had been no cinch for him either, and he told me that after Peleliu, he was told to pack his bag and go down to the airfield to be flown home for a thirty-day leave. He was standing by for the plane when word came, canceling all further departures. And he hadn't been able to see his family in almost four years. I found later that it took several stiff drinks to loosen John up to his former happy-go-lucky self.

The week of boondocking being over, we heard a critique by the division commander, Maj. Gen. Pedro Del Valle, and other top officers; held a whale of a hard-drinking party for infantry and artillery at our own officers' club; and tried to catch up on some of the lost sleep. That was a real party, with a hot dice game in which a New Zealander "who had never played before" cleaned up. Some of the bunch from the Fourth Marines dropped down from their end of the island, Jamieson, a big blond Princetonian among them, and we sang ourselves hoarse following his lead on "Alouette." A puffy-looking doctor from the Fourth became exceedingly tight and began swearing he had the straight dope that we were going to hit Okinawa Gunto and that our casualties would be terrific. We shut him up.

The next day, the first Sunday in February, a great Battalion picnic was held for officers and enlisted men. We enjoyed hamburgers, beer, and fresh corn on the cob from the Guadalcanal plantations, then a plunge in the delightfully cool river. After we had dressed, the men had fun throwing all the officers back in the water.

By the end of that week, February 10, 1945, we had returned by LSM to Pavuvu in the Russell Islands. And then came the final preparations. The maps of the Ryukyus were hauled out in the protection of our officers' mess. One by one, we covered the welter of mimeographed and printed data about those islands, the aerial photos, and the blue lines that indicated our beaches. The men would not be told until we left our staging area.

The guns were freshly painted in camouflage suited to the Okinawa landscape. Rear-echelon gear was marked and collected. New combat equipment was drawn for all individuals. All hands were plugged with one hypodermic injection after another. Gas masks were tested. Combat pictures of Peleliu were shown. And long inventories for combat loading had to be worked out, as I well knew.

Despite this fury of preparation, I was sent out to another island to practice with the armored amphtracks, firing them as batteries of 75s from one island to another. At other times, Williams, Perkins, and I and other FOs spent the day on an amphtrack directing the fires of the new M-7s. We almost burned up, sitting out in the broiling sun all day long on an open metal tank. One could feel all moisture leave his body.

I was now tenting with Dr. Wetzell, a teetotaler, and our Assistant Battalion-2, Captain Wilcox, who was just as likely to go to bed with a bottle of whiskey. I was still drinking very little but had secreted a few bottles in my combat gear. By February 10, we had received the complete Decca volume of the Broadway musical *Oklahoma!* I was charmed by the album; so was Major Wooster.

A series of farewell parties were given. NCOs were invited to one, the officers of a transport in the harbor to another. At the former, there were fights among the NCOs. At the latter, Duplantis came over, swiped one of the Navy officers' caps, and borrowed my best fountain pen, a Schaeffer, which I forgot to get back that evening. Grass passed out cold on a mess table, Gibson tried to close the bar on time, and Emery cursed him for it. Gibson swung on Emery, and Colonel Roe threatened Gibby with a court-martial. I stood up for Gibby, and Colonel Roe shouted that he would have me up for a court-martial, too, if I dared "to try to run his Battalion." Thus did our tensions break in the streams of liquor and beer. A lot of people were already thinking of that high seawall and those concrete tombs shown along the Okinawa beachfront.

The last Sunday in February 1945, I took my team of one scout corporal, two radiomen, and four wiremen down to the dock. We rode across the channel by barge to the beach where armored and personnel amphtracks were being loaded into the belly of *LST 982*. On the sides of the LST hung four gigantic metal pontoon rafts. On her upper deck perched a fully assembled LCT. My men were given choice accommodations on cots under the stern of the LCT. When George Company of the Seventh Marines came aboard, I shared a stateroom with Huff, Gunnigle, and Lieutenant Smith. Including the amphibious tractors' officers and crews, we had just over 400 men on a ship with normal passenger accommodations for 120, now cut down to about 70 because of a hospital unit that occupied the port compartments. Of course, the officers and crew of the LCT lived in the quarters aboard her.

Other LSTs were loading in the same manner at the Pavuvu beaches. The First Division filed slowly aboard with full equipment, all bound for Tulagi. By the next morning, we had anchored among the numerous islands of that prewar center of British rule in the Solomons. A vast fleet of troopships of all descriptions had gathered into these now safe waters, where twenty months before I had first seen a ship (an LST) sunk by a full-scale Jap air raid. Not far from our anchorage was beached the sternless bow of the LST on which part of the Ninth Defense had traveled to Rendova.

The business at hand was organization of the detailed plan for practice landings. We carried in the LST's hold six armored amphibious tractors and eight personnel amphtracks. The former were to act as a mobile assault artillery until the beach was reached, while the latter carried the first and second waves of troops. I was assigned an amphtrack with my own FO team, a squad of riflemen, a mortar squad, and several corpsmen and stretcher-bearers. We were really jammed in, as we discovered later.

There was a tremendous book that was passed about for all officers to read. It contained every detail of the landings, the ships scheduled to take part, the kinds of snakes to be found on Okinawa, how to treat civilians whom we captured, and what curios were worth buying. The "Okies" were supposed to have a high venereal rate but little malaria. Typhus was said to be bad, and snakes especially numerous and virulent. I was happy to have my leggings for once and envied those who possessed boots.

The first practice landing gave me an idea of just how fouled up one of these affairs could be. We rose early and were in the amphtracks by 0630. When the bow doors of the LST opened to disgorge us, we were off Cape Esperance at the northwestern end of Guadalcanal. On the left of the First Division were the ships of the Sixth Marine Division. As the amphs left the LST, they circled. First, the armored vehicles pulled off to form the first wave with armored amphs from other boats. Then, the amphs of the first troop wave and, next, the second troop wave attempted to join up. The Slot was choppy that day, which gave our coxswain plenty of trouble in spotting the wave guide. After we had circled and bobbed and sweated under the tropic sun for an hour, half of the boys in the boat were sick over the side. We started from the line of departure some thirty minutes late, some two hundred yards behind the first wave of troops. The wave guide, a Navy lieutenant in a launch, proceeded to give us a bum steer, so that we landed a full five hundred yards up the beach from where we should have hit. The first platoon of the company landed down the beach from where they should have, which rather effectively split the unit. We then perspired on the beach until we could be picked up and taken back to the LST. Here, we had the fun of catching a rope ladder, in order to hoist ourselves aboard while the LST heaved up and down.

The next afternoon, we obtained shore leave. Gunnigle, Huff, and I shopped at some of the naval PXs and finally wound up at the Tulagi Officers' Club, high on a hill. We drank beer with hundreds of others from the many ships in the bay. I saw officers like Bill White, E. Davis, and others whom I had not met in months. Several passed out from an excess of spirits and had to be carried down the steep hill to be dumped into launches and carried back to the ships; unable to climb rope ladders, some of them were hoisted aboard in cargo nets.

The second practice against the Cape Esperance beach was preceded by a bombardment from destroyers and rocket ships. It proceeded more on schedule and gave us a chance to set up radio contacts between the FO team and the amphtracks for simulated artillery fire. The contacts were not too satisfactory because of difficulty with the tractors' radios. We also were unable to run wire through Gibson as liaison to our Battery. When we arrived back on the LST that afternoon, the young lieutenant in charge of the personnel amphtracks was missing. He had last been seen by his sergeant, strolling alone up the beach toward Cape Esperance. Some days later, we learned that he had been picked up, stark naked, in one of the huts of the native village near the Cape. He had evidently gone somewhat off his nut.

With rehearsals out of the way, our LST headed back up the Slot for Pavuvu. We took on a few additional supplies there the next morning. I made a hurried trip to our Battalion area by hitching a ride in a jeep. My mission was to find my bedding roll, in order to bring it aboard as the other personnel had done. Only one or two tents remained standing in the entire regimental area. It looked as if the camp was already reverting to the jungle, whose noises hummed its funeral dirge. Unable to find the bedroll, I returned to the beach, where I met Golden, the CO of A

Company, Seventh Marines. He told me that Duplantis still had my "life-time" Schaeffer pen, which he wanted to return to me. I said that I would pick it up the next time we were near one another.

Within a few hours, we were back at Tulagi. More ships had gathered to form an impressive armada. Captain Norton bought beer for every-one and had it placed in the ship's hold, while Huff and I visited a naval recreation hut and talked the administration into allowing us to select seventy-five Pocket Books for the men.

Our First Division's group of LSTs set forth from Tulagi about March 10. For the fifth time, I said good-bye to Guadalcanal (always one of my favorite occupations in the Pacific). We headed north and then northwest.

It was now that we fell into the real shipboard routine that was con-cerned externally with the varying position of the sixteen ships and three destroyer escorts of our convoy and internally with our thoughts of what was to happen, of home, and of those onboard with us. Huff, tall and skinny like me, had been a law student in Georgia. He was conscien-tious about his work as Battalion-2, always ready to pass on a bit of dry humor, and he loved his "sack time" on shipboard. Gunnigle, a Brook-lyn lad, recently married, also a law student, was tall, well-built, and gifted with Irish wit. He was attached to the Second Battalion, Seventh Marines' Headquarters, as naval gunfire observer. The three of us had started at Quantico the same day and so could shoot the breeze on many matters, especially the vital question of when we might expect promo-tion. In the fourth bunk of our cabin was a big man, Tom Smith, former head of a union of a New York steel concern, who had started as an iron miner and had that sort of physical constitution. He had been wounded once at Peleliu, but he was still a platoon leader.

Tony Janick, who had been in the Thirteenth ROC with us, was the Exec of George Company. O'Mahoney, Warren, and Mason were platoon leaders. Lieutenant Boudreaux of Louisiana, a big, good-looking, dark-complexioned man, was in command of the armored amphtracks on-board our LST. He and I mapped out a plan by which I should observe fire for them after we had hit the beach. There was also a pint-sized but competent major who was the executive officer of the Second Battalion of the Seventh Marines. He liked to argue that after we had cleaned up Germany and Japan, we should go right in and mop up the Soviets. I told him that we would have had enough fighting by that time. Although outranked, Captain Norton was troop commander, and a damned effec-tive one, whom the NCOs and men loved.

The Marines mentioned were a group, sticking closely to one another. The Navy men who sailed the "long, slow target" and the officers of the LST topside messed together in the small wardroom before we ate our chow. They were all a good lot, driven rather sternly by the skipper, a young lieutenant commander, a reservist enjoying his first command, who carried out naval regulations even to the period of daily calisthenics. (He was handsomely muscled.)

At least fourteen hours of the day we spent in the sack, sleeping, reading, writing, or chatting. We dined in the wardroom, tried to brief the men under our command, listened to phonograph records, and played poker with just about everything wild. The last mentioned was for small stakes, and I was able to play many nights before losing my maximum of $25 and staying out. Huff, Gunnigle, and I plugged the recordings of music from *Oklahoma!* and *Porgy and Bess.* We thoroughly enjoyed the humor of "Po'r Jud is Daid," although Mason always shouted for us to turn it off.

Before going aboard, I had received *Night unto Night* by Philip Wylie from Madge. I read it and mulled over some of its ideas and satirical points of view. When Norton finished it after I had, I heard him comment, "Why did I have to get hold of something like that at such a time?" One of the ship's officers had three of James Cain's works, which all of us gave a rapid perusal. They seemed sordid, but they stuck, and they were potent enough to take our minds off the ever-nearer future. The shipboard interval also gave me time to read Ben Franklin's *Autobiography* and *Revolt in the Backlands* (Brazilian).

George Company had a large plastic relief map of the section of beach we were to hit. This was placed on deck, where we could use it to brief groups of enlisted men. We could see the seawall whose height was not accurately known but furnished a psychological threat. (The assault platoons were furnished with long ladders to aid in scaling the obstacle.) We noted the town of Sobe, four hundred yards inland and our objective for the afternoon. There on the left flank was Yontan airfield to be taken by the Fourth Marines. And on the beach, just at the left boundary, was a little bunch of rocky land jutting out just far enough to give enfilading fire along the beach line. But, then, the armored amphtracks were to neutralize that quite readily. I pointed out to Ganz, Monahan, and the others of my team how we should proceed, when the wire would be laid, how we might have to keep low at all times if fire were directed at us from the two-hundred-foot-high ground overlooking the beach. They took it with a grin.

Before March 20, our convoy sailed into the great advance naval base of Ulithi Atoll. We streamed in single file through the hundreds of ships of every description anchored there and finally found our assigned area in which to drop anchor, not far from two beautiful, white hospital ships. During the first night at Ulithi, there was an air raid alert, and several planes were said to have been shot down many miles outside the atoll. Last-minute information was given, and we received the most recent combat maps of Okinawa. Then one big event occurred—I believe it was Palm Sunday—when the aircraft carrier *Franklin,* her decks blackened and shattered, sailed by us into anchorage. The disastrous bombing, which had gutted her, had occurred only a few days before.[4]

We never went ashore at Ulithi. From what I could see, the shore wasn't much wider than the deck of a big carrier. So, the beer remained untouched in the ship's hold. The chaplains came aboard on the last day at this staging area. In the narrow corridor-like compartments of the LST, they heard our confessions and said Mass in a room so jammed, one could scarcely see the priest. I joined in the confession and communion, yet I had been doing much thinking about religion during the voyage and questioned whether any single religion could form an adequate channel for my spiritual course.

We snaked out of Ulithi the beginning of the last week in March and almost immediately hit very foul weather. The edge of a typhoon had apparently enveloped us, making it difficult at times to spot other ships in the small convoy. During clearer periods, one could barely discern the sixteen or so LSTs of the Sixth Marine Division now far astern. The gigantic waves tossed us about like twisting sticks and slapped against the huge metal rafts hung alongside. The LST in advance of us lost one of these seventy-five-foot pontoons, which we barely managed to avoid. Water continually poured over the gunwales and almost swamped the cots of the men bunked beneath the stern of the LCT. On occasion, when the rain let up, I attempted to hold a meeting of my team to discuss the maps and other details. But if five or six attended, before fifteen minutes had passed, all but one or two found their way to the rail. So I sought them in their bunks and passed on the "dope."

I was feeling in good spirits now. I had the sense of having put all my affairs in order and of being ready to take a part in something really big. There were many unpleasant things that might happen to a member of an assault wave if the enemy met us in strength, but what good would it do to worry about them? There was no altering the fact that I was committed, and with a great organization to back us, things might go smoothly. Besides, despite predictions that we might lose 50 percent on the beach, I had a hunch about this time that the Nips would not be happy about the preinvasion bombardment, and I even told my team that perhaps they wouldn't meet us at the water. There were other pessimists who forecast an early attack by Jap tanks and bemoaned the fact that our own armor wouldn't get in until the fourteenth wave.

In these last few days, weapons received loving care: knives were sharpened, automatic weapons test-fired over the side, and carbines cleaned. I had planned to carry a light pack ashore with poncho, field glasses, map case, gas mask, and carbine, with jungle knife, ammo, and two canteens on my belt. Now, I added seven feet of green tablecloth of the type used in covering pool tables and wardroom tables. After the cool nights I had experienced in Hawaii, I wanted to be ready for chilly nights in place of the tropic weather. I also carried a pint of whiskey. The beer began to disappear from the hold and by the last day of March, it was all gone. Since naval regulations did not permit its being distributed on shipboard, a lot of looking in the other direction had to be done. No one became tight, and the men at least had their last fling.

On the afternoon of March 31, the sun appeared, and the Pacific became Pacific. At suppertime, while the Navy was at mess, there was an alert to "general quarters." The officers rose from their seats as a man and started on the double for the wardroom exit. But the first man, the skipper, slipped and went down, with seven others all piling on top of him. What a sight! And, naturally, we couldn't show the discourtesy to laugh until they had unscrambled and gone to stations. No planes appeared.

That evening, we heard distant thunder and looking eastward in the darkness saw the tracers and star shells of what we knew must be the battleships bombarding Okinawa. During the day, we had received reports from the underwater demolition crews as well as the latest photos of the beach. Evidently no new obstacles had been set, and the old ones had been cleared without opposition. It sounded hopeful.

A restlessness gripped the men that night; they roamed the ship, listened to the radio reports, and always returned to watch the distant lights of the shelling. I tried to turn in early, realizing I would need every bit of energy on "A Day." But sleep was very fitful and often disturbed by the others who couldn't sleep. The tune of "Easter Parade" drummed ironically in my mind.

CHAPTER 4

April 1 to April 12, 1945

The Easter Sunday landings on Okinawa with the Seventh Marines; supporting the 383rd Infantry of the Army's Ninety-sixth Division at Kakazu and Cactus Ridge

Breakfast was served at 0330 on April 1. We received oranges, cereal, steak, potatoes, boiled eggs, and coffee. I ate heartily of as much as I could and then stuffed a couple of eggs in my knapsack. Everything was checked and rechecked, ready to go. It had been decided that I should take my entire FO team in Norton's amphtrack. He wanted artillery support right on hand.

We watched for the dawn, cruising in the roll of a quiet sea. All crews were at general quarters. I stood on deck in the darkness. Suddenly, there was a far-off rattle of automatic fire, a burst of light off our starboard bow, and a plane aflame crashed into the water half a mile away.

At 0530 the drivers went below to warm the motors of the amphs. At 0600, as someone on deck sang, "Oh What a Beautiful Morning!," we donned our gear and filed down the hatches to the tank deck, ducking and crawling from the top of one amph to the next. I brought my team into Norton's amph, but by the time he had arrived, it was evident that conditions would be too crowded. He recommended a split, and I left him three wiremen while taking my scout Ganz and two radiomen into another amph of which I assumed command. Several stretcher-bearers had been added, making this vehicle so crowded we could scarcely turn around.

At 0630 the ramp doors opened and the winch let down the ramp. One after another, the armored amphs clattered into the water, followed by the personnel carriers. Each group cheered as they left the bow.

As we splashed into the sea, I was aware at first of only the brilliant sunlight and the rolling waves, and of the deafening roar of big guns. In the heavens were planes and more planes, squadron after squadron of fighter-bombers wheeling about on a great circular course. A Liberator[1] flew low all over the place, evidently having something to do with direction of the landing activities. When I looked about me at the seascape, I felt as if this were a harbor. LSTs were everywhere, and farther out were transports coming into position. But the sight that gave a thrill, that really made it a great picture, was in toward shore, where a line of battleships and heavy cruisers, cruisers and destroyers poured salvo after salvo at the enemy shore. We couldn't see the coast; it was completely beclouded by smoke.

We were put-putting in a circle now, men perched on the high sides of the amphs waving at men in the other craft. We saw the armored amphs form a line and head for the line of departure; then the first wave of personnel carriers, and then ours. More than twenty other waves would follow us that day.

I could spot no enemy shells landing anywhere among our ships. And now, as we began to move forward, we could see the squadrons of fighter-bombers dive for the beach and release their eggs. New clouds of dust and smoke rose from the shoreline. Using glasses, I could discern the outlines of fields and hills through the haze. By now, the armored amphs were six hundred yards in front of us, and we were cruising along slowly. Directly in front of us loomed the gigantic USS *Idaho*. We used her as a shield from shore until we came right under her port side, amidships, and skirted around her fantail where her after-gun battery crews cheered us with shouts of "Good luck" and "Give the bastards hell, Marines!" We moved abreast amidships on the starboard side, just under a battery of fourteen-inch guns. As we headed for shore again, this battery let go with a salvo whose blast rocked us. In the muzzles' flashes, I could see the instant black silhouettes of shells.

Now we were committed, with two thousand yards to go. Beach Blue No. 1 was in front of us, being given its last strafing by our fighter planes. I could now see the coast clearly and was amazed by the steep slope of the hillside, for those hachure lines on the map had seemed relatively far apart. Through glasses, I could see the seawall and the entrances of several tombs.

I ordered the men down from the sides of the amph and told them to stay low. It was at this exciting moment that I saw one of them hunched up, reading a comic magazine. As we passed a rocket ship, now firing away with its automatic weapons from 600 yards out, I saw the armored amphs blazing away with their 75s and 20s on the last 200 yards of their dash for the beach. There appeared to be nothing coming our way, but I put my head below the armor as we opened full throttle for that last 600 yards. There was no chatter now. Each man's face was tight, teeth set. Even above the roar of the amph's motors, we began to hear the crackle of small arms from the beach.

We hit with a jolt that tumbled us in a heap, and ground up onto a coral shelf, then onto sand. The stern ramp dropped, and as some of the infantrymen swarmed over the sides, I led the rush out and onto the beach. We had hit a small nose of coral jutting out from the rest of the coastline, and I estimated it must be the little point some three hundred yards north of our proper beach. I immediately brought my team against the shelter of a seven-foot cliff, told them to wait there, and clambered up the side to reconnoiter. Fifty yards inland, setting up a barrage of rifle fire, a wave of Marines advanced standing up. As I looked back again at the shoreline, I could see a few of our amphtracks mingled with many of the Sixth Division and realized that we had positively missed our beach through some error of the driver. Where was Norton? Deciding to go forward and bear to the right, I called the four men of my team to come on. We began to run up the hill after the advancing infantry, who were still blazing away at every bush or hole in the fields of vegetables. One of my radiomen was exhausted by our speed of advance after some five hundred yards of this hill climbing, and I had to take over half of our heavy radio set in order to keep them going. I was feeling exhilarated that there was as yet no enemy action, only slightly concerned about our confusion in landing.

At last, after moving almost one thousand yards in and some two hundred yards south, we found G Company's headquarters group, and I joined Norton. A broad grin expressed his own pleased surprise at the ease of this landing. He agreed that we were still several hundred yards to the left of our intended zone of action, but he told me that he was swinging his two advance platoons, now already on the edge of the airfield, over to the right.

In a few more minutes, we had reached Yontan and saw a mass of junked Japanese planes at one end of a runway that was not too badly scarred by bomb and shell craters. As yet, there was no report on my wiremen who had been in another amphtrack. As we reached the far side of the airfield, a heavy patrol of the Fourth Marines came up to us. They were amazed to find our company here, for they were supposed to be the first unit to take this section. I had attempted to make radio contact with either the armored amphtracks or our Battalion liaison, Gibson, but so far I had been unable to effect it. Everyone was too much on the move.

Just beyond the principal runway in front of the village of Irammiya, we took a breathing spell and broke into our rations for lunch. A little later, as we began to move in single file through this first truly oriental town I had ever seen, two infantrymen drew forth from the ruins of a house a decrepit old man, clad in black robes, his chin trailing a long, scraggly white beard. Many of the houses were still standing, though it was evident that their tile roofs and their wooden walls had all been riddled by steel fragments. Each structure possessed its front and rear court of fruit trees or shrubs, while its privacy from its neighbors was ensured by tall hedges. Within these courts, we saw a number of new Jap fighter planes, carefully concealed from above by natural forms of camouflage. Some planes had been hit; others were in excellent condition.

Beyond Irammiya, we held up in a narrow valley covered by rice paddies as Warren's platoon fired into a cave in the hillside. One squad had heard voices within the cavity and had used military Japanese to tell whoever it was to come forth and surrender. When no one moved out, the squad opened up with BARs. Two men, a woman, and a three-year-old boy were found within, only the child alive, but covered with his mother's blood. They brought him back to us, and Monahan washed the blood off the boy, who had ceased to cry. My team carried him on their shoulders all the rest of the afternoon, until someone could be spared to take him back to the Civilian Control camp at the beach. So this was Easter Sunday warfare—it sickened me by its pitiful aspect. Still, no sign yet of my wiremen.

We advanced now by a small road; passed motorcycles that had been ditched by the Japs; found bridges knocked out. As we came up a hill, we met units of E Company and discovered my missing wiremen with the other FO team. I asked for Johnny Williams and was told the sorry news that as he and Captain Beardsley were climbing out of their amphtrack at the beach, a shell had hit in front of them. The latter's grenades had been exploded around his waist and tore him up badly enough to make death certain, while John's head had been bloodied. (Beardsley had widowed the girl he had married on his thirty-day leave only a few months before.) The amphtrack had immediately set off for its LST with the two casualties. Williams's tall, young wire corporal, Jordan, had taken charge of that FO team and had laid wire all the way along the advances.

My own wiremen claimed that the amphtrack that carried them ashore pulled off so quickly that they had been unable to unload the reels of wire. I was infuriated by this failure and by their subsequent failure to keep up with Norton. But at least we were together safely, and I made arrangements to tie into the other wire team's line.

The unit came upon a group of long, low buildings, which were evidently troop barracks. Straw mats were spread along platforms that ran the length of the buildings. The smell was the unmistakable odor of fish and rice. I found some paper forms, one of which looked like a day-by-day muster roll, which had been kept up through March 22. I presumed the troops had been withdrawn then.

We made one more hill and then received orders to dig in for the night because the Fourth Marines on our left were falling behind on that flank. This hill or ridge, some five thousand yards from the beach, had a gradual rise on the reverse slope and dropped away precipitously in front for a hundred feet or so. The land then rose rapidly to high hills overlooking ours.

The time had come for me to shoot in my barrages for the night. I moved forward to the crest and had Monahan set the radio up below me. At last, we managed to contact Battalion FDC, which reported that one battery, H, was ready to go, and requested that since I was the only FO with whom they then had contact, I should shoot in all the barrages for as much of the Seventh Marines' front as I could see. But my vision was limited to the ground in front of our two advance companies. I was frankly worried anyhow about this first big shoot on my responsibility. Norton came up for a look and suggested a shallow draw between the high hills in front of us. He didn't know where we were on the map. I sent down my own dope, and the round wasn't fired for a half hour because Battalion went through all sorts of channels to get clearance from Division. Then, just as they reported "On the Way," I caught sight of a double column of civilians coming around the bend of a road on the opposite hill. More than two hundred were in view by the time my round landed not very far away from them. They fled and disappeared as I called for "cease-fire." When minutes passed and they did not show themselves, I made an adjustment and fixed "concentration 101"[2] for the Battalion.

It was now sundown, and as I tried using code to send Major Wooster some report of troop positions, we heard the throb of airplane motors and the rattle of machine guns. Five or six Jap fighters skimmed over us, low to the ground, and headed for the harbor. Looking up from our flattened position, we saw a terrific shower of tracers go up from the ships offshore and thought that we noticed two planes crashing. In a few moments, the excitement was over and the air patrolled by an American squadron of F6Fs.

It was pitch black before I could assign our watches for the night and eat a few rations before digging myself a very shallow trench near the radio. All was quiet as I covered myself with a poncho and went to sleep, tired but thankful that we had met no resistance.

Near 2:00 A.M., I awakened to the noise of artillery shells. At intervals of two minutes or so, they whined overhead and exploded somewhere a short distance in front of our position. Each one sounded awfully low, but not like a 105 mm, though definitely coming from our rear area. I was feeling acutely uncomfortable now from the icy chill, which seemed to grip the hills. The ground and my poncho were dripping with cold dew. My joints ached.

Suddenly, there was a terrifically loud whistle, and a flash of exploding shell illuminated a part of our company position this side of the ridgeline. In a moment, another fell on the ridge. I immediately radioed Battalion to report the occurrence, asking them if any of our batteries were firing. They were not, was the reply. By this time, an infantry officer crept up, whispering my name. He was excited. No one had been hit, but fragments were all around. Was I firing? Would I cease fire? Another landed on the ridge. I made a rather frantic appeal to Battalion to find out who was firing short and have it stopped. In a short while, the shelling ended.

By now, it was my turn to take a watch. I sat by the radio until 0500, reporting to Battalion liaison every thirty minutes and rubbing my hands and knees to stimulate circulation. Every few moments, a star shell would light the heavens with a brilliant white, which painted objects on the ground a silvery hue.

We resumed the advance early in the morning, climbing a series of hills. We took turns lugging the heavy radio packs. In the first half mile, we saw two dead Japs in incomplete uniform sprawled by the side of the trail. A little further along, a column of civilians, mostly women and old men holding on to one another, came running down the dirt wagon path. A few of the stronger ones had their arms laden with personal belongings. They were unkempt and frightened. When some Marines said hello and made an offer of candy bars or cheese rations, the natives only hurried on faster, the older women tugging at the arms of the girls, as if in fear of an assault.

By noon, we had made more than a mile when we were held up at a bend in the trail, where it climbed around the outside of a hill. Hearing rifle and grenade fire, I moved up to Norton and asked him what he was doing. Evidently, some guerrilla fighters were engaging our left platoon in a gully. While Norton was following this on the "spam can" radio,[3] I tried to find our position on the map. He couldn't help me in the matter, so I climbed cautiously up the eight-foot bank of the path and looked over the landscape for landmarks. Seeing that I was on a level field and noting a small bomb crater some forty yards ahead, I walked briskly out to the hole and plopped into it. A couple of bullets pinged overhead, and another hit the earth in front of me. I looked to the rear and was able to make out our men hugging the ground along the top of the bank. After a few minutes of laying low, I stuck my head up enough to use the glasses. About a thousand yards forward were two low hills parted by a shallow, winding ravine. In front of these was gently sloping, scrub-covered land. I noticed a column of troops in single file, some twenty in all, appear from woods at the left front and start across the sloping ground. Then, by looking at the map, I was able to estimate my position. I ran back to the shelter of the bank. The captain asked how I liked being out in front of our line. I protested that I had just seen one of our patrols several hundred yards in front. Old Norton was excited immediately and declared that we had no troops there. He obtained more powerful glasses, and we dashed up to the shell hole. The column was nearing the hills. "Hell," he said, "it's the bastards who have been holding us up on the left. Can you get us some artillery in a hurry?"

My radiomen ran the set out to the crater because we couldn't see the enemy from the bank. I sent down the mission, calling for time fuzes. A first round was fired for adjustment and landed to my left about on a line with me. Colonel Berger immediately came on the radio from his Battalion OP and ordered us to cease fire. (I later learned that the grid and distances on our maps were several hundred yards out, causing a short.) Norton argued with the CO, and after ten minutes we had permission to go on firing. Of course, the Jap troops had by now disappeared into the ravine, but my concentration of five volleys of time bursts[4] between the hills was just right. Without the delay, we might have seen some results.

The resistance on the left apparently had been chased off at the cost of one slightly wounded, when a question of zone of advance arose back at Regimental Headquarters. We relaxed while this was being thrashed out, when suddenly mortar shells began to drop all around us. We hit the deck, breathing hard. Every time we thought they were over and would start to rise, a few more would drop in. We could only guess from the trajectory that they were coming from the neighboring Sixth Division. How we escaped injury is hard to say.

Just at this point in the afternoon, a coded message came through from Colonel Berger to prepare to fire at certain coordinates. When I looked on the map after decoding it, I couldn't believe my eyes: the spot was on the Yontan airfield. Norton was baffled but showed me a high spot on the flank from which we could see that part of Yontan. Looking through his glasses, we saw a tremendous activity of vehicles racing about in swirling clouds of dust. We were surmising that a counterattack on the strip was feared, when Gibson radioed that his men had used the wrong code for the day and that what Berger really wanted was registration on a given point to the front, which would help him determine the boundary of advance for the Battalion.

We moved only five hundred yards in the remainder of the afternoon, as Fox Company under Captain Grass passed through us and over to positions on the left flank. I shot in normal barrages for the night and slept deeply in a green, soft ditch. My team and I finished my pint of whiskey.

By morning of our third day on Okinawa, Captain Haislip had been sent to Easy Company as FO. Norton's company was now pulled into reserve, but my team was ordered to join Fox Company. We arrived on the scene of a tragedy. Six corpses, all Marines, were covered on the ground. There had been noises during the night, and one boy, going rather berserk, fired at anything he saw moving before he himself was laid low. Captain Grass was embittered over this needless loss. The entire outfit moved heavily. We moved up and down the steepest parts of the highest hills in that sector. We sweated it out under a terribly hot sun, trying to keep our heavy radio along with the infantry. On one ridgeline, we met sniper fire every time we moved. The bullets sang merrily overhead. Now, we had been informed that resistance was coming from Okinawa home guard outfits.

There was a frost that night that had us all shivering under our ponchos. My hand froze just holding the radio mouthpiece for the usual thirty-minute reports. From the highest point that day, we had been able to see the other side of the island, but it had looked as if the vehicles of the Army to the south of us were already there. But on the radio we heard Sigler and other members of Item Battery's FO team reporting that they were pinned down by Jap machine-gun fire and had two casualties. Toward nightfall, they managed to pull out.

The fourth day on Okinawa was just a marathon along the roads until we reached the sea at the town of Ishikawa and then turned south for a mile in front of Hizoana village. Patrolling the beach, we frightened a large family of civilians who, not trusting us, took to their heels. I used some textbook Japanese on the rapidly disappearing figures, something equivalent to "Halt, or we'll fire!" One old man stopped and turned, and then hurried on after the others. They were pitiful people, dressed in fluttering, black robes.

We made camp on high ground overlooking the beach, and for the first time in four days, I took my shoes and clothes off. We bathed in the bay. During this procedure, more than fifty civilians came out of a cave in the beach cliff and turned themselves over to our guards. We later discovered that one man spoke English. He informed our Battalion intelligence officer that all the Jap soldiers had left the island ten days or so before the invasion began.

I put my team in the small, grass-covered court of a tomb, where we enjoyed the unusual luxury of shaves, ate 10-in-1 rations passed out by Fox Company, and then slept as much as possible during a drizzling rain, which had us soaking wet by morning. The advance across the island was over; it had required three and one-half days instead of the estimated fourteen. We had suffered a few casualties, but the units were in full force. But where were the Japs?

On April 5, as we moved back from the beach, orders came to dig in, in preparation for an airborne counterattack. None came; instead, we gathered sweet potatoes and eighteen-inch radishes and made a vegetable soup. On the following morning, my team was ordered to meet the other FO teams at the destroyed sugar mill of Hizoana, from which we were driven back by trucks to the Battalion's position.

For almost three days, we took it easy, washing the few articles of clothing that we had and enjoying the first hot food in a week. On the second of these days, I took the supply sergeant and a recon truck and headed for the landing beaches. It was amazing to see the traffic on the roads and the supplies pouring ashore. We found our way somehow to the Eighth Amph Battalion and talked one of the officers into taking us out to my LST, which I had been able to spot from shore, even though the waters were jammed with more vessels than I think I have ever seen in one place before. While we were waiting for the lift, an air raid siren sounded and all hell seemed to cut loose from ship and shore guns. The sergeant and I just lay on the sand and watched as two Jap planes circled the harbor at fairly low altitude. I saw one blow up before it could dive for a ship and lost sight of the other. The raid was over as quickly as that, and the terrific din of AA quieted. The old LST looked completely different, with the deck entirely bare and the pontoon rafts removed. All our seabags, I found, had been moved ashore. I looked up the LST's first officer and talked him into letting us take about eight cots, a can of yeast, and one hundred pounds of flour. The galley meanwhile fixed up a couple of steak sandwiches.

On shore again, I managed to find my seabag among some other stacked-up gear. I added what articles I could discover that belonged to my men, and we returned to camp, coated with a half inch of dust. Bill Miller welcomed the flour as an asset to the battery's mess. I was surprised to find that Johnny Williams had returned to the unit, despite the fact that the back of his neck was all taped up. He said that the raids on the fleet had been terrific, even when he was on a hospital ship. (He was hit by a bomb a few days later.)

On the evening of April 8, we had our first definite word concerning the Army. They were not in Naha but were meeting resistance north of that city. We of the Third Battalion were to be the unit to move down in support of the "dogfaces" of the Army's Ninety-sixth Division. Indirect support? No, direct! When? Tomorrow. Who were to go up as FOs? The same six teams of the Battalion. We packed, feeling exceedingly disgruntled at having been chosen for this Army job.

We moved out with all guns and gear on the morning of April 9, traveling over the dirt roads through the small, wrecked villages, southeast through Chatan to the East China seacoast. We followed the coast along roads already being bulldozed until we reached the neighborhood of Isa. At this point, Haislip, Miller, and I were dropped by the roadside with our FO and liaison teams. A battery weapons carrier was assigned to carry us forward. As we waited, subdued by the contemplation of what might be ahead, a horde of more than a hundred civilians walked down the road escorted by military police. They trudged along, the old women with shrunken breasts dangling loosely from unfastened kimonos.

About four in the afternoon, an Army jeep arrived to guide us. My team took its turn in the weapons carrier, and we rolled painfully along the crater torn "highway." After two miles of this, as we came within sight of the town of Uchitomari, several large shells burst across the road a short distance ahead of us, setting a house on fire. The driver jammed on the brakes, and I turned to tell the men to lie low, only to find them already in ditches along the roadside. That welcoming salvo appeared to be all, and we continued into the village, which was now burning brightly in several sections.

Miller, Haislip, and I were soon ushered into the presence of the CO of the Army's 383rd Regiment on the outskirts of town. A young staff officer, at the colonel's request, drew forth a map and began to brief us. Evidently our front lines were now in open, level ground at the edge of a valley leading between two hills and up to a third, on the other side of which was the village of Kakazu. This morning the regiment had advanced to an intermediate high point, had even gone part way up Kakazu hill, but had been blasted off and retreated to its earlier position. Tomorrow morning, there would be another attempt to take the valley and hill under cover of tremendous and well-planned artillery fires. The Marine artillery would be assigned to various companies and engage targets of opportunity. We should have the pleasure of going right along in the assault. It all sounded beautifully planned: as if its success was a foregone conclusion; as if the failure of that day had been merely a technical error.

Miller, Haislip, and I summoned our teams and followed a guide up a winding trail to a point high on the reverse slope of a precipitous hill, called Cactus Ridge, just inland from Uchitomari. Here was Second Battalion Headquarters of the 383rd. Miller remained there as liaison, while Haislip went over to one company, and I joined another. This company, of which the captain was a slim, wiry, dark-haired fellow, occupied a position around the left, forward nose of the hill. The CP was inside a rather large tomb.

When I arrived, the captain was on the point of holding a powwow with his officers in their observation post atop the hill, where they were awaiting him. We chatted as we climbed up through rocks and brush. He told me of the battle they had had two days before in taking this very same rock pile. It had eventually been necessary to use almost the entire force in a frontal assault, and losses had been heavy. A moment later, we came upon the scene where the Japs had offered their last resistance. At least two dozen torn and bloated bodies lay about, with individual sections, such as an arm, a lower leg still in a shoe, or a head, lying off by themselves. They were all Nips. The stench of death was very strong. The captain, walking ahead of me, bent and picked up a bloodless hand. He held it out to me as if he had found a piece of jewelry: "This must be the hand of my mess sergeant!"

Three very young lieutenants met us at the top in a small cockpit among the rocks from which he could look out across the valley toward Kakazu. I noted a small road, which I thought I could identify on the captain's map. He gave a very formal order for operations on the succeeding day. It may be unfair to say so, but it sounded as if he wanted this Marine to know that he could do it by the book. At any rate, I guessed the going had been plenty rugged because the young officers took it all in, and seriously. And no one put his head up much beyond the rim of the cockpit.

The captain pointed out a tree-lined bank four hundred yards forward as being the present forward line and the morning's line of departure.

We returned to the company CP, ate a can of rations, and retired for the night. I was amazed to discover that the entire company had managed to find some form of tomb or caves as cover. After some discussion among the officers, it was decided that I could take my team into a cave on the forward slope, already occupied by a mortar outfit. We arrived there at dusk. A sentry sat in front of a hole. The cave behind it was nothing more than a narrow tunnel, not even high enough for a man to sit upright, which burrowed into the hill for fifteen feet, dropped three feet, and ran back another twenty-five feet. The pitch blackness of it was packed with mortar men. We wriggled ourselves across their bodies to the rear, only to find the floor of that section a mass of dust and sharp rocks that made it an agony to lie on. We finally set the radio up just inside the entrance, where the mortar men gave us room, and I rolled up in a blanket on the ground in front of the sentry.

About 8:00 P.M., I had my first introduction to Jap mortar fire. The brilliant flashes and roars began in the valley. Then our own mortar flares went up every few minutes, lighting the same valley area. I fell asleep for a few moments after this, until another heavier barrage landed nearer to us up the slope. When this stopped, I heard some big shells whine overhead and land not so far behind us. Some of them seemed to strike about the hilltop. The next salvo of mortar fire was so close in front of us that I could hear fragments overhead and see the sentry's face illuminated. When I saw him creep inside I, too, wormed my way into the tunnel mouth and toward the completely darkened-out rear, apologizing to every face I stepped on. A moment later, an explosion just over our entrance brought down a shower of rocks, dazed us with the noise, and filled the cave with cordite fumes. There was no more sleep for the remainder of that night as, time and again, salvos burst outside the tunnel's entrance and shook rocks loose upon us inside. I took a radio watch and greeted the dawn with relief as the enemy's firing ceased.

The Army mortar squad packed their gear, after a hasty breakfast, and shoved off for the line of departure. I met the company commander and kept my team with him. We utilized every form of cover in making our way down the forward slope of the hill although a thick mist reduced visibility.

Our small group reached the bunker that formed the line of departure, just at the time scheduled for attack. Infantry were everywhere, occupying hundreds of foxholes behind each and every ridge or mound of earth. These were farmlands somewhat terraced, with a footpath running along each bank of soil. A few trees along the predominating bank helped to screen the assembled forces. An occasional shell could be heard to crash against the forward slope of this barrier.

The captain left us behind a low bank and went up to the front line. Three or four puffs exploded a few minutes later in the area that he had traversed. I ducked down to keep out of this mortar fire. In fifteen minutes, the captain returned, saying the attack had been delayed, but that we could establish an OP on the front line where he might be able to point out one or two targets.

I told my radiomen to accompany me, and we ran forward to the higher bank. At the right end of this, we found a slight depression between two shrubs, in which we were hidden and yet able to peer over the top. There was a shallow alley in front of us, with some low cliffs twenty feet or so in height, about two hundred yards across from our position. The face of these cliffs had obviously been blasted by shell-fire for some time. It was the forward slope of Kakazu Ridge. The captain called my attention to a cave opening directly in front of us. As we watched, we saw the muzzle of a field gun protrude, fire, and disappear behind rocks. The shell blasted into our front line. I asked him if he could estimate our position on the map. He couldn't. I could only hazard a guess, but I had to know accurately, with the target being so close.

We made radio contact with Battalion FDC. They said that Haislip had fired a concentration in that area early in the morning. They fired it for me—one round of smoke—but I couldn't pick it up. The next three adjustments were also lost. I was sweating over this trouble while the artillery fire, mortar, and rifle fire from both sides were rising to a crescendo and obscuring much of the landscape in smoke. Then I saw what I believed to be our round. I adjusted closer and to the right. It landed almost on the nose of the cave, and I fired for effect. It was a half hour before the gun stuck its barrel out again—undamaged. Meanwhile, the captain left to check on his company, which was still waiting for the word to go.

And now, as I again started to send a mission to FDC, our radio went dead. We tried several tests without any luck. I decided to try to find Miller and use the liaison radio. To my surprise, they had moved into foxholes just behind us but were having difficulty with their own set. I decided then that I should find the captain and let him know of our failure. I thought him to be a hundred yards or so down the line to the left. A footpath ran in that direction. I took it, ran thirty yards, and saw bullets dig up the dust almost in front of me as I heard them slap hard into the earth. (That had been a Nambu machine gun.) I jumped back off the path and began to circle more toward the rear, passing among a number of infantry in foxholes and by the wire team of our own George Battery. Just then, there was a warning shout of "Mortars!" I looked up and saw them just above—big stuff. One hit almost beside me, and I went down with the blast.

Something that felt like a baseball bat had socked my right arm over the biceps. I think I said aloud, "I'm hit! This is it!" My head was ringing. Someone was helping me sit up, asking me if I was OK. I looked at my arm. No blood, but a piece of steel was sticking out of my flannel shirt. I grasped it and pulled it out, almost burning my hand as I did so. Then someone said, "You better get a medic," as blood began to ooze out. Then I looked around rather dazedly and saw others stretched on the ground with medics administering aid. Two Marines were down, one with a bad gash in his back. More mortars fell nearby as I ran back to the OP and told my radiomen to get in the best foxholes they could find. Then I rejoined Miller to catch my breath. As the corpsmen were busy and the bleeding had stopped quickly on my arm and leg scratches, I paid it no more attention. The captain happened by in a few moments, and Miller explained that I had better stay with him until we could obtain some form of communication.

A drizzling rain commenced. We covered ourselves with ponchos and waited—waited for the infantry to attack. Meanwhile, by using some parts from our FO team's radio, it was possible to fix the liaison set. Miller was asked to join in firing a barrage on the high ground to the front. This would precede the attack. For forty minutes, Miller fired in concert with the Army's artillery. The din was terrific, and the enemy-held hills were cloaked in smoke and dust. Still, the troops of the Ninety-sixth Division did not move. We were asked to repeat the barrage. After another twenty minutes amid a downpour of rain, the infantry got up from its foxholes and advanced slowly down into the valley. Scattered machine-gun fire came from the Japs. The "attack" bogged down almost immediately before it reached the cliffs two hundred yards in front. Several men, slightly wounded, struggled back, calling for medics.

Apparently, a flanking move was made on the left about 2:00 in the afternoon. One company succeeded in advancing there along a road and across a stream for about four hundred yards. Battalion Headquarters' troops were given the word to move up to support this position. (We heard that the Battalion was already far under strength.) Miller told me to bring my men with his. We fell into single file behind the heavy mortar squad and slowly moved along the path behind the main bank until we came to several buildings grouped at a crossroads. We had to wait thirty minutes beside the largest building, which was obviously a school, a frame structure built around an open court. As the rain again became intense, I took my men into one of the classrooms. The furniture, handmade desks, had been damaged, but I found several books in good condition, including several English grammars and readers.

Suddenly, several heavy shells landed on the other end of the school. We dashed outside to see that end burst into flame. The rain extinguished the blaze. The shelling continued and made us seek cover behind a three-foot-high grassy slope across from the school. We were now at the intersection with the school at our backs, the main road at our left. Across the main road were two private homes. Several big shells crashed into these houses, and a moment later, a mortar man ran across the road to us, begging for stretcher-bearers to take out six wounded men from the houses. Two of his squad, he said, had just been killed. To bear out what he reported, another infantryman, his hand streaming blood, came across the road supporting another man who had been painfully gashed in the buttocks by shell fragments. They moved none too quickly as Nambu bullets kicked up the roadbed and then spanged into the ground above our heads.

There were four stretcher-bearers who had come up behind us and were lying in the shelter of the bank. The mortar man saw them and shouted to them to go across to the houses. But the men rose, not touching the stretchers, and began to run in the other direction. The mortar man pulled out a pistol and yelled that he would fire if the "bastards" didn't return. The men came crouching, then ran across the road with their stretchers amid more machine-gun fire from some sniper up in the hills.

More shellfire came dangerously close, again hitting the school. It was obvious that the enemy had good observation on this intersection. Word came back that the road ahead was impassable. The infantry company's Exec told Miller to move us back. In thirty minutes, we were back at the bunkers where my team had had its first foxholes of the morning's action.

Night was closing in; wind and rain chilled us thoroughly. My arm was throbbing and stiff. Repeated salvos of enemy mortar fire kept us close to the ground. Miller and I dug a hole together, but it was too short to allow me to stretch out. We covered it with a poncho, which collapsed under a weight of water during the night. Miller slept exhaustedly, snoring. The water was four inches deep on my side where I sat, my teeth chattering, and my body involuntarily wracked by shivers as a cold wind began to blow away the rain. It was one of the longest nights of my life.

Dawn was dulled by swirling fog. In the half-light, I could see a shack to our right rear, in which it looked as if a small fire might be burning. I made my way along the bank for the hundred yards to this shepherd's hut of straw and brick. Sure enough, two young soldiers had kindled a fire in the old earthen oven and were both cooking tinned eggs and coffee and drying clothing. The fire seemed to give everyone a spark of life, but I asked if it could be seen. They claimed it was too far below the mask of the forward lines. I then took some rations and hot coffee, which made me feel a lot better, and warmed up my socks and shoes.

The sun rose higher. Suddenly, there was a burst of Nambu firing, with bullets whistling close to the hut. We hugged the ground. When we looked out again, we saw that another soldier, who had been standing on the bunker, had been shot through the rear.

Miller came over for some coffee, and soon the entire outfit was on the move. By midmorning we found ourselves back at the school intersection. One at a time, allowing twenty-yard intervals, we ran across to the houses where the mortar men had been hit; then, we moved from house to house, paralleling the road until we reached an open field; crossed to houses on the other side; sneaked through their blasted shells; and then made a dash over a fully exposed section at the head of the bridge to get out of sight beneath its left side. Two or three snipers appeared to be concentrating their fire at this point, for every man who made the dash was a target. I was now bringing up the rear of our FO teams. After the last of our men had made it, I let out with all speed, heard a couple of whining sounds, but found myself safely across. A moment later, I heard a spit, a curse, and the soldier who had been following me tumbled down beside the bridge with a shattered right shin. A medic took charge of him. Beneath the bridge, we found Haislip and his team where they had spent the night, safe at least from shellfire. We followed downstream, across a wall and into a tiny triangular field, the front end of which was protected by a forty-foot cliff—the east end of Kakazu Ridge—tunneled with several caves. On our left was a wall, which separated us from another narrow valley that held the Battalion CP. On top of this cliff were the infantry's front lines. In other words, everything was jammed together. There was no prospect of the infantry attempting to move forward. The

Japs were holed up on the rear slope of the ridge and held most of the crest on our right.

We had just established our radio when the Army FO, a good-looking lieutenant who had climbed the cliff to an OP, had his leg shot away by a Jap 47 mm gun, and he toppled down the steep slope. They carried him out, but he was the last one to be evacuated. From noon of that day, no one came in or went out. The pocket was again sealed by Jap artillery and machine-gun fire to our rear. Other men were wounded along the top side and even toward the rear of this fifty-by-seventy-five-yard depression. They were given first aid or a little better by the Battalion doctor and placed on stretchers and were laid in foxholes next to us. Three became delirious. One died. No water or rations reached us that night.

By sundown, Miller and I had established an OP on the sharp ridge to the left rear of the Battalion CP. We could crawl up the last ten feet on our bellies and stick our heads up among some bushes. By the time we had a wire hookup with the radio, we could only fire in a normal barrage and let it go at that. The Nips, we were sure, occupied another ridge three hundred yards to our left front, from which they could see the entire road.

We dug in deeply for the night, Miller and I sharing a much longer foxhole than the night before. The Jap artillery dropped round after round at the head of our valley, showering us with dirt and pebbles, but we remained low enough to escape injuries, though those soldiers who had stayed only thirty or forty yards back of us suffered several casualties. But, we were sufficiently exhausted to sleep soundly between volleys.

Early in the morning, we manned the OP. We had the sun over our left shoulders. Suddenly, Miller told me to watch a certain cave opening in the opposite precipitous cliff wall. In a moment I saw what he meant: the sun flashed on two glass disks in the darkness of the cave mouth. The disks moved together. It was a Jap OP. Because the opening was not more than four feet and was flush with the vertical wall, Miller decided that it would be a difficult target for artillery. On his orders, I sought the Battalion CO in his own cave below us and asked him for a bazooka man who could use direct fire from our ridge. The CO, who had suffered a slight wound, stated that if his man used a bazooka, the Japs would spot him and blast him off the ridge. We eventually worked out a plan whereby we would fire salvos of artillery at one-minute intervals, and just as the bazooka man heard each salvo coming, he would let go. We tried it, after waiting a half hour for the bazooka fellow. We fired five volleys, twenty rounds, above the cliff, and all we saw was one puff near the edge of the cave. I crawled over to the soldier and asked him why he wasn't firing on each volley. I could have torn my hair when he replied that his battalion had only two rounds of his ammo. The first had been a dud, and the second had missed.

Miller then fired a beautiful firing problem using a single 155 mm howitzer. On the twenty-first round, the face of the cliff above the cave was crushed, falling and closing the opening. We collaborated on some of the adjustments.

There was no change in the situation for the remainder of that day. The infantry stayed put, having thus far failed to take Kakazu. The Nips continued to pound us at times with mortars and heavier shells. Occasionally, a man was hit. Sniper fire covered the road to the rear, although some water was brought in at sunset, and it became possible to evacuate the wounded that night. Again, we lay low as the Jap barrage increased with darkness.

In the morning came the rumor that the Army's Twenty-seventh Division was moving in on our right, that they would replace this unit of the Ninety-sixth. What would happen to us as FOs? At last, Battalion gave us the word: "Pull out." A truck would pick us up where several days before—it seemed ages—we had arrived at the front. We gathered our gear, bid the Ninety-sixth good luck, and ran single-file back the same route for more than a mile.

We were positively overjoyed to see the two Third Battalion trucks. We were headed back to the safety of the Battery. Sigler, Perkins, MacDonald—in fact, all the FO teams and liaison teams of the Third Battalion—were there. Sigler had had to man an Army machine gun in the lines when the "Doggies" withdrew for a time, thinking a Jap counterattack was headed for their weakened outfit. We all agreed that a real Nip counterattack against that regiment might have found little strength. But we had seen only a few Jap bodies and couldn't believe there could be as many as the Ninety-sixth Division had claimed.

We drove back down a road crowded with vehicles and the first units of the Twenty-seventh Division moving up. Our Battalion was established between the coastal railroad and the road where some deep cross-ravines offered fair protection for men's shelter halves and a few large tents. The guns were being fired when the trucks rolled into the otherwise peaceful scene. Suddenly, before we had even unloaded from the vehicles, the sound of motors roared low overhead. I glimpsed two Jap planes roaring by, even as all of us scrambled over the truck's sides. AA fire immediately filled the air above us, the large black puffs close to the ground. Shouts came from the open ground just above the ravine into which the vehicles had turned. "Corpsman, corpsman!"

A corpsman and a doctor ran over, and I followed. One boy was lying on the ground. It looked as if his right leg was almost severed from his body near the hip. Another man near him was also down, and further over, a second lieutenant was holding his eye. A low-bursting naval shell had caused these casualties after it failed to hit one of the enemy planes. Another had penetrated into the tent of a medical unit across the road and had taken off the head of a clerk seated at a table.

This was our "safe" welcome to the peace and quiet of the battery after days at the front.

CHAPTER 5

April 12 to May 6, 1945

Acting "Exec" for Battery H; FDR's death; serving as FO alongside F
Company of the Army's 106th Regiment, Twenty-seventh Division,
at Hill 58 and Yafusu; Company F is relieved by the First Marines

It was after our hectic return from duty with the Ninety-sixth Division
that Colonel Roe made his decision to give all battery officers a turn at
the FO duty. From then on, he was no longer a merely unpopular man: he
was hated by those who thought of themselves as safe behind the guns.
Not one of the officers was actually scared to go up, but they felt that certain consideration was due their previously assigned tasks. We who had
been up could foresee a long and welcome "rest." That night, I crawled
into the cot that I had brought from the LST and slumbered exhaustedly,
my ears still ringing madly from the mortar blast and my entire arm black
and blue where I had had my "vaccination." We took shelter from long-
range artillery only two or three times before morning.

The next eight days were a hodge-podge of activities and changing
"dope." I began now to help Dick Woods "Exec" the battery. Missions
were very few and far between because the Army was sitting still, gathering strength for an assault on Kakazu Ridge.

Six of us now dug in a pyramidal tent for shelter: Miller, Haislip, Gibson, Williams, and I. We really enjoyed the nights when we retired early
after chow and lay in our sacks, with the light of one or two candles,
discussing the Battalion, the campaign, and home—especially the last.
President Roosevelt's death during this week hit everyone.[1] The big question was raised in our minds: Would it change the course of the war?
Would the latter be any longer or shorter? Two correspondents from Chicago papers visited us there in the tent one night. Someone brought out
a bottle, which loosened tongues almost too much, for my fellow officers
began the old business of damning the "dogfaces." The correspondents

swallowed that and said little on the subject. Then, they told us that the Navy had called off the plans for hitting another island further north. Forty destroyers put out of action by kamikazes in the first ten days was too discouraging a toll to permit another similar operation. And, besides, it looked as if there might be several more weeks of fighting on Okinawa. Those correspondents looked far more tired than we; they were on the move a lot more, had even less sleep than we, and sometimes were close to hot spots.[2]

About April 17, I rode a truck northward on the island to the beaches and to the headquarters of the Seventh Marines. Their headquarters were still around the village of Ishikawa, which they had partly burned for no particular reason. And the day we went up, Fox Company had run into a small ambush, which cost them several wounded. We saw no one we knew intimately and failed in our objective to find some of the belongings of members of the FO teams that had gone unrecovered since the landing. Stopping at the Army salvage center later on, however, we succeeded in convincing its CO that having served with the Ninety-sixth Division, we should be given buckle boots and blankets for all members of our FO team.

In these days, too, when there was time out from Exec duties and writing letters, I strolled along the funny narrow-gauge track of the coastal railroad or poked around in some of the deserted homes. A large sow had moved into one of the better dwellings, where she defended herself and her brood against all comers. We were under orders not to kill any livestock, although a story was then current that General Del Valle had invited the Army's Lieutenant General Buckner to a dinner of suckling pig. Buckner, the Tenth Army commander, had eaten several helpings and subsequently put his host on report for violation of this island-wide order. In any case, whether this story was or was not well-founded, we heard enough semiofficial dope to let us know a battle was in progress at Tenth Army Headquarters over the part that the Marines should play in this battle of South Okinawa, now that the First and the Sixth Marine Divisions had almost mopped up all the northern section. Curtailment of plans for a new landing in the northern islands of the group certainly was good news, but it made the Marines quite available.

In my first ramble along the railroad, I noticed a basket within which, wrapped in paper, were eight saucer-sized blue china plates. I stuck them in my seabag because I admired the design and color.

Meanwhile, each officer in the Battalion—except the two colonels—

was taking a turn on the line doing nothing. There was no firing at close range, little artillery work. The Japs directed their big stuff at the rear, mostly at night. The new roads going forward, however, were crammed with soldiers and supplies. Things were being whipped into order for the proposed big breakthrough across Kakazu Ridge and the Urasoe-Mura Escarpment. It happened on April 19. But instead of rolling, gathering speed, and overrunning the island as the Twenty-seventh Division had promised, the movement crashed forward less than a mile and bogged down. Somewhere in the center, they had hit Hill 196, and everywhere in front, the Japs had the high ground overlooking that sparsely covered terrain. The drive stopped cold as it reached the northern edge of the now worthless Machinato airstrip. It was another four days before the attack again ground forward.

In the meantime, Michevich had been retransferred to H Battery, Williams was ready for duty, Captain Haislip was ordered to QM work, and Miller expected the FO duty to be restricted to the junior officers in the battery. It looked as if I could count on exec work.

On the night of April 27, Haislip produced a farewell bottle of Jap alcohol that he had obtained from Motor Transport. We were enjoying "highballs" of the firewater mixed with grapefruit juice when the phone in the tent rang. I was told to report at once to Battalion Headquarters at the FDC.

I made my way through the blackness into the gully and was ushered into the presence of Colonel Roe. He told me very briefly that word had just come that Sigler had suffered a concussion from a near miss and had been taken to a hospital. I was needed to take over that FO team by morning. The usual briefing was done. Lieutenant Swanson gave me maps, pointed out gun target and other data, and wished me luck because it had already proved to be a rough spot.

When I returned to the tent, the party was over, and Miller and Williams were saying what hard luck it was that Sigler had been put out and that I had to go up. The old stuff! I packed all my gear by candlelight. (In case the outfit moved, I wanted everything of mine to go along.) Then, having readied a light haversack and blanket and feeling very much alone, I hit the sack for a few hours' sleep.

The colonel's driver took me along the coast road before dawn the following morning, April 28. We bounced along past Uchitomari, past the intersection of the trail leading to Kakazu, across an engineers' bridge over Machinato stream, just before reaching the village of Machinato, which was completely destroyed. The main road curved to cut between the sea and the end of the abrupt Urasoe-Mura Escarpment. We took a trail which brought us to some tombs at the base of this escarpment.

The sun was just rising as the driver and I crept into one of the crypts to awaken two radio operators of Regimental Liaison. One of them, on my orders, contacted the FO team and found that two men were leaving the front lines to act as my guides. We then had tinned rations for breakfast and waited. Within forty minutes, a corporal and a private clambered down a trail on the face of the ridge. After a brief rest, the three of us started up the same steep footing. As we neared the top, a terrific stench of rotting human flesh assailed our nostrils. On the bare hilltop were several score of Jap dead, some badly dismembered, and most of them in contorted, bloated shape. The dead faces stared up hideously, while the odor really made us take short gasps of air through our mouths. We continued to see more of these unfortunate enemies as we followed a twisting trail through a shell-blasted woods, which covered low rolling hills of red clay. The sound of artillery and small arms fire increased.

My guides eventually showed me where they had been two nights before. From there, they could point out the present position of the FO team on the reverse slope of a low rise about three hundred yards forward. We covered about one thousand yards, however, to reach that spot, moving along the embankment of the single track railroad line which came in at our right and ran in that direction. The Japs were constantly throwing in mortar fire of a harassing nature, which kept us moving rapidly. We could see a couple of stretchers being carried out on the run. Upon arriving at the FO post, we were told that one stretcher carried the radio operator, who had been hit in the leg only ten minutes before our arrival.

I was now standing where Sigler had become incapacitated—behind a low rise that did not afford enough cover to permit a man's standing upright. About 150 yards to our right, on the other side of the railroad embankment, was a narrow sloping hill, which rose to a seventy-five-foot crest overlooking us. A couple of short valleys and hills to the front prevented observation in that direction, except where I could see the railroad track cutting through those hills. To the left, the land rose to what was a small-sized mountain at the middle of the island's girth.

I introduced myself to the CO of the infantry company (I think his name was Captain Sweet). He said he was glad to have artillery at hand and asked me to concentrate on the hill to the right, Hill 58, next to the town of Yafusu, unless I should find 150 yards too close for artillery fire. I felt at the time as if I could reach out and touch the damn hill, from which came occasional bursts of Nambu machine-gun fire. But I felt suddenly eager to help, and finding that I had wire communication with Battalion, I crawled over the rise that constituted our front line and quickly eased myself into a hole on the forward slope. Immediately, it began to drizzle rain. I covered my phone and began to study the hill through field glasses. An infantryman five yards behind me made some comments about the weather to me, stood up in his foxhole to adjust a poncho, and was hit in the shoulder by a sniper's bullet. I crawled over and helped another infantryman to remove the man. When, a little later, I wanted to register on the hill, Battalion told me that it was unsafe because our troops were supposedly already on its top. I told the major that such was scarcely a true picture of the situation, but I was not then allowed my mission. So, this company of the Army's 106th Regiment, Twenty-seventh Division, received little of the artillery support that they needed at the moment.

The FO team was Sigler's from Item Battery. The scout sergeant, who was really a gun section man, had volunteered to come up to the lines for the first time. He was a good boy, full of wit, and his observations about how little he liked this type of duty kept us laughing. As the wet afternoon wore on, he spelled me in our forward OP.

About 1500, things began to happen in earnest. Orders came through to take Hill 58. Evidently, the company from the Battalion on our right had failed but was thought to have softened up the objective, which might be more approachable from our side.

I laid a small barrage, therefore, as near to us as possible as allowed by FDC. It was about three hundred yards in front and landed over the far end of the hill. The assault began with some of the troops dashing across the railroad tracks and hiding behind a low bank of earth. The next boys who tried it met with machine-gun fire, as did everyone who moved in that area. I believed that I could detect wisps of smoke or dust from a dark spot in the steepest part of the hillside about two hundred yards from us. When I called FDC, the major objected, but I explained the urgency of the mission related to the attack, and he obtained permission to adjust with one piece. I was on with the third or fourth round and fired for effect. The area of the dark spot crumbled satisfactorily, and the automatic fire appeared to have been stopped. I was glad because within a half hour, I had to move my team across that track, and the mortar and rifle fire coming our way was enough without the Nambu. But where such a target is the focus of attention, an artillery FO can seldom claim it as his own prize because our own automatic fire and mortars were being directed at the same area.

In short dashes of twenty-five to fifty yards, we moved with the company headquarters through a road cut across the base of the hill and lined by subterranean rooms. Then between the wrecked houses of the village of Yafusu and slowly up the right side of the hill to a cleared area about half-way up the short slope. The infantry had already cleared the low summit and were still firing and hurling grenades into the several cave entrances at the side and top of the hill. By sundown, the position had been organized defensively; I had brought up wire communication, crept forward to the summit, and found a second crest seventy-five yards in front of me blocking most of my field of observation. I was told by a "listening post" detail that we did not yet possess the brush-covered knoll in the immediate foreground. I tried to register my barrages for the night as close to the rear of that knoll as possible, but I lost most of the rounds until I shifted well to the right. About that time, a lot of knee mortar shells[3] landed all around us. I went back to the FO team, who had dug their holes for the night. Feeling unhappy about my inability to get good observation, I made arrangements with the captain, dug a shallow trench in the hard ground, ate some beans, and lay down.

The night was filled with our star shells whistling up from the cruisers and battleships. Every few minutes, shells would roar overhead. Mortar fire landed to the left and right of our hill, but the company remained unharmed.

The next morning, April 29, was bright and sunny. Supplies were brought up by the Army while we dug our OP a little deeper. Several bodies lay about the hilltop. They appeared blackened, as if they had been seared by fire. One, half buried in rubble, had a face rendered almost indistinguishable. We crawled over him several times to reach the OP and thought nothing of it until an Army detail discovered that he was an American, which caused us remorse for our indifference. (As I think of it now, I realize how little compassion we had even for the enemy dead. Combat had reduced our humanity pretty close to a matter of nationality.)

To our left, we watched another company, with Gibson as FO, move around to our old position, pass through our rear, and work around our left flank across the railroad again to a knoll above the railroad pass. They suffered several casualties from rifle fire, and I became aware that several high ridges to our left front afforded the enemy excellent obser-

vation of this area. It was my first view of the high ground in front of
Shuri, still at a range of about four thousand yards from our present
position. Our planes were bombing and strafing that area quite often
during the day.

With afternoon came the order to advance. At the same time a short
round from another artillery outfit so jolted Captain Sweet that he had to
be removed. Two platoons were sent out, one on either side of the hill. I
was told that no barrage would be used. As the units, each no more than
twenty-five strong, converged on the brushy knoll to our front, there
was no firing of any kind. Then, as they were walking erect and only a
few yards from the bushes, they were suddenly met with blazing light
machine-gun fire, and mortars began raining upon them. It was sudden
and devastating. There was no cover. They were too close to the small
clump of bushes for any support to be given. They fell, squirmed, and
were hit again. A handful managed to get back, including a lieutenant
who trembled and shook with terrific sobs, murmuring over and over, "It
was awful, God, it was awful. They all died."

I felt awful myself. Those few minutes had just about wiped out the
fighting strength of the company. I reported the grim details to FDC.
There were obvious caves in that brushy knoll from which the Japs had
poured out their deadly fire at twenty-five yards and from which they
had sent out the mortar shells in almost perpendicular flight. I had seen
the men clutching the air, wriggling to find any bit of raised earth as
cover, and screaming, cursing, or crying. But no one could help. We went
on the defensive again; we dug in deeper.

Earlier in the day, the FO teams had been changed. I had received one
from my own battery, led by wireman Sorenson and including a sixteen-
or seventeen-year-old Navy corpsman, two radiomen, and two other
wiremen. The company to our left had received a team in command of
Lieutenant Fullmer. At this low point in our fortunes, the big, burly, red-
headed acting CO of our unit was visited by the CO of the left flank company, who brought over the other FO, Fullmer, who was relatively new
to the situation. I had met him briefly when he joined just before leaving
the Russells and again as we returned from the "siege" of Kakazu. Now,
we planned defensive fires for the night, knowing that little reserves
remained to throw against any countermove from the Japs.

Lieutenant Fullmer and the other company's CO returned to their
unit. Over the wire, I could hear the adjustments of the other team. Then
the message broke off—followed by the excited voice of the radioman

telling FDC that Lieutenant Fullmer had been shot through the stomach by a sniper. (He was removed by stretcher as soon as possible, already becoming delirious, but pleading his bearers to make his men keep their heads down. This father of two children died that night.)

At dusk, some cases of rations were being brought up from the rear when the enemy must have spotted the movement. He landed eight or ten heavy shells in the area near the base of the hill, killing several of the bearers. All afternoon, the same sort of heavy stuff had been trying to hit some of our tanks, which were attacking a quarter mile to our right over by Machinato airstrip. We slept very fitfully in the hard rock holes on the hillside. We had heard that our right flank was entirely unprotected, for the Battalion on that side had not been able to advance across those open fields.

In the morning, after a miserable breakfast, I talked to the company's Exec. He told me that he was receiving aid from four tanks for an expected attack. The men were gathered in small groups and briefed on the action. They were a dirty, tired, disgruntled lot of men—impressed by their own small numbers. The tanks were an hour late, and these were only two with an M-7 armored vehicle. The mechanized force rolled gingerly out of Yafusu, skirted the side of our hill, and blasted away at the brushy knoll. One tank lumbered up the side of the hill onto the saddle between the two hills. As it approached the brush, it managed to slide into a muddy ditch where it stuck, in full sight of the heights before Shuri. Within a few moments, several heavy shells plunked against the side of the hill, and the boys in the tank scampered out of the useless weapon.

Now the infantry began to move forward, one man at a time, scampering from rock to rock or other form of cover. The Exec's OP was next to mine on the crest. I observed that the men were not laying down any base of fire with their Garands. He thought it was a good suggestion and shouted orders, which resulted in more rifle and tommy-gun fire.

The other tank and the M-7 were in and out. There was no teamwork with the infantry because there was no communication except beating on the turret of the tank or shouting at the M-7. But they succeeded in rolling up to several cave mouths and in blasting into these with cannon and machine guns. Then the infantry enveloped the knoll seventy-five yards in front of us. No Japs were in sight.

I immediately decided that this was my chance to move my OP forward of the brushy knoll and thereby obtain more favorable observation. Leaving Sorenson at the phone, I took my carbine, crossed the saddle past the

Captain Christopher S. Donner, First Marine Division, in photograph taken at war's end. (Christopher S. Donner)

French barracks at Noumea, New Caledonia. (Christopher S. Donner)

Lt. Col. William J. Scheyer (shown here as a colonel in April 1945), the CO of the Ninth Defense Battalion in 1943. (U.S. Marine Corps, Quantico, Virginia)

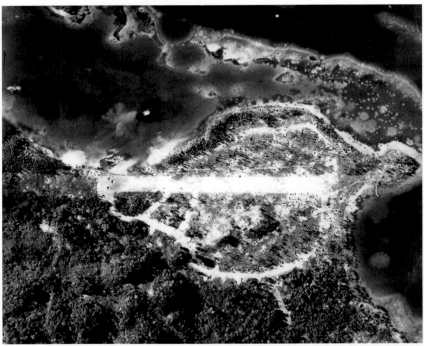

The Japanese airfield at Munda Point, in a photo taken in July 1943, the intended target of the Ninth Defense's "Long Toms." The horseshoe-like features below the airstrip are revetments for the protection of planes from U.S. strafing. (NARA)

A Ninth Defense 155 mm "Long Tom" rolls ashore from an LST on Rendova Island in preparation for the bombardment of Munda. (NARA)

"Murderers' Row": Battery A's 155 mm guns in action on Rendova. (NARA)

Black Friday, July 2, 1943: A 2½-ton truck smolders after the Japanese air raid. Note Battery A ("A-6") marking on the truck's bumper. (USMC)

A near miss: Smoke from a Japanese bomb that landed nearby drifts over a Battery A "Long Tom" near Suicide Point, July 2, 1943. (USMC)

A Battery E gun crew stencils enemy flags on the barrel of their 90 mm gun after the July 4, 1943, raid, in which Battery E set a record by downing twelve of sixteen Japanese bombers with eighty-eight rounds. Platoon Sgt. Robert Wattles does the painting, while Lieutenant Colonel Scheyer holds the stencil; at far right is Battery E's CO, Capt. William Tracy. (NARA)

A damaged photo of the Ninth's tormentor, "Pistol Pete," after its capture on Baanga Island. (NARA)

Loading and firing one of the 155 mm Group's Long Toms. (NARA)

Munda Point airfield after its seizure on August 5, 1943, and reopening of the airstrip by Seabees and Marine aviation units. Compare this photo with the aerial photo taken in early July to gauge the full extent of the area's bombardment by the shattered palm trees. This view is taken from Bibilo Hill. (USMC)

Maj. Robert C. Hiatt. This photo was taken of Hiatt as a lieutenant colonel on Okinawa in 1945, as he tested a pair of captured Japanese Nambu heavy and light machine guns. (USMC)

Chris's tentmate and A Battery's executive officer, Charles E. Townsend, in front of an English-made washbasin on Nusalavata, fall 1943. (Christopher S. Donner)

Taken in early 1944 in the Ninth's "R&R" camp on Banika in the Russells, this depicts half of A Battery, 155 mm Group. In the inset, Donner is at the far topmost right corner; half-standing in front of him is his CO and fellow Philadelphian, Capt. Henry H. Reichner Jr. (Christopher S. Donner)

Lieutenant Donner in field uniform, autumn 1944. (Christopher S. Donner)

CO of the Third Battalion, Eleventh Marines, Lt. Col. Thomas G. Roe, in 1945. (USMC)

The invasion fleet at anchor on the evening of "L-Day" on Okinawa. *LST-70,* in the right foreground, was reputed to have fought in every seaborne landing operation in the Pacific. (NARA)

Marine LVT(A)-4 armored amphtracks, such as the one on which Donner served, lead the first invasion wave on Okinawa, Easter Sunday, April 1, 1945. (USMC)

The initial landings on L-Day were virtually unopposed. Here, Marine infantry-men, accompanied by an LVT and a M4 Sherman, advance inland. (NARA)

This oblique aerial photograph shows the initial landing beaches, the zones of demarcation between the two Marine divisions (First and Sixth), and Yontan airfield, where G Company of the Seventh Marines would meet up with elements of the Fourth Marines. (USMC)

An aerial photo of Yontan airfield. (USMC)

Above: Nighttime firing by a camouflaged 105 mm howitzer. Note the crew avoiding the muzzle blast, which lights up the camouflage net and extra ammunition stacked nearby. Photo by Cpl. L. V. Eastman. (NARA)

Left: This photograph captures two Marine FO team members in action on Okinawa. (USMC)

"Miller then fired a beautiful firing problem using a single 155 mm howitzer. . . ." A Marine 155 mm howitzer in action on Okinawa, crewed by section chief PFC R. F. Callahan. (USMC)

Taken on June 18, 1945, this is the last photograph of General Buckner, CO of the Tenth Army (on right), at a Marine forward observation post minutes before he was killed by Japanese artillery. Only days before his death, Buckner had similarly appeared at Donner's FO position. (USMC)

"'With that?,' I asked, pointing at the BAR." A Marine automatic rifleman in action on Okinawa with his BAR near Naha, June 5, 1945. (NARA)

"Two tanks with liquid fire poured it into cave mouths:" A flame-throwing Sherman tank accompanies Army Ninety-sixth Division infantry in reducing a Japanese strongpoint. Photograph taken in June 1945. (NARA)

Marines in action on a ridgeline two miles north of Naha on Okinawa; photograph by PFC Lewis Giffin. (NARA)

The remains of Shuri Castle after its seizure. (USMC)

Marine observers on the heights overlooking Naha. (USMC)

"A barrage of all artillery on the island convinced us at noon that V-E Day had arrived." Two days after V-E Day, the war continued in earnest on Okinawa: Here, First Marine Division troops watch a white phosphorous barrage fall on the hills outside Naha. (NARA)

The blasted terrain of Wana Ridge. (USMC)

Dakeshi Ridge, partly shrouded in dust thrown up by a bombardment. (USMC)

Although depicting a Sixth Marine Division demolition crew, scenes like this one were common sights for forward observation teams like Chris Donner's during the fighting on Okinawa. (NARA)

Three generations of an Okinawan family receiving medical treatment from a medical corpsman with the Marines. (NARA)

Chris Donner upon his return to Mt. Kisco, New York, from the Pacific, with Madge and Toph. (Christopher S. Donner III)

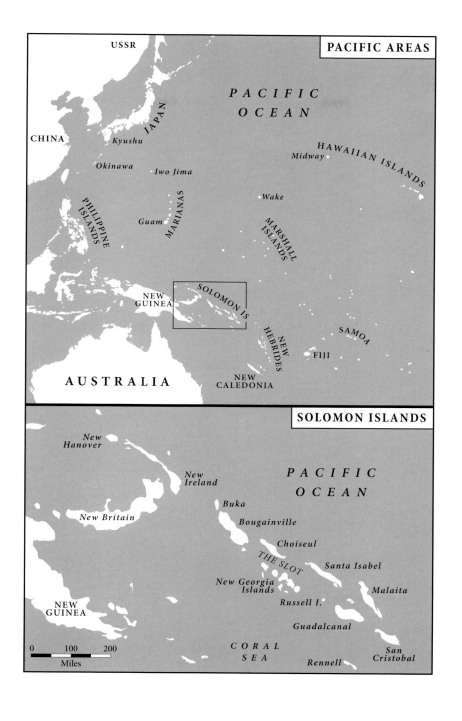

PACIFIC AREAS

USSR

PACIFIC
OCEAN

CHINA

JAPAN

Kyushu

HAWAIIAN ISLANDS

Midway

Okinawa

Iwo Jima

PHILIPPINE
ISLANDS

MARIANAS

Guam

Wake

MARSHALL
ISLANDS

NEW
GUINEA

SOLOMON IS.

NEW
HEBRIDES

SAMOA

FIJI

AUSTRALIA

NEW
CALEDONIA

SOLOMON ISLANDS

New
Hanover

PACIFIC
OCEAN

New
Ireland

Buka

New Britain

Bougainville

Choiseul

THE SLOT

Santa Isabel

New Georgia
Islands

Malaita

Russell I.

NEW
GUINEA

Guadalcanal

0   100   200

Miles

CORAL
SEA

Rennell

San
Cristobal

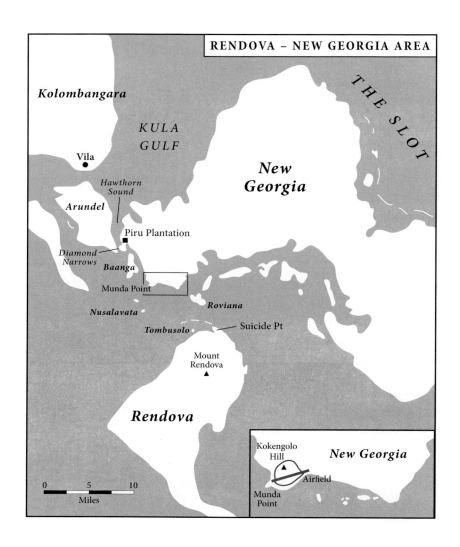

RENDOVA – NEW GEORGIA AREA

Kolombangara

THE SLOT

KULA
GULF

Vila

New
Georgia

Hawthorn
Sound

Arundel

Piru Plantation

Diamond
Narrows

Baanga

Munda Point

Nusalavata

Roviana

Tombusolo

Suicide Pt

Mount
Rendova

Rendova

0   5   10
Miles

Kokengolo
Hill

New Georgia

Airfield

Munda
Point

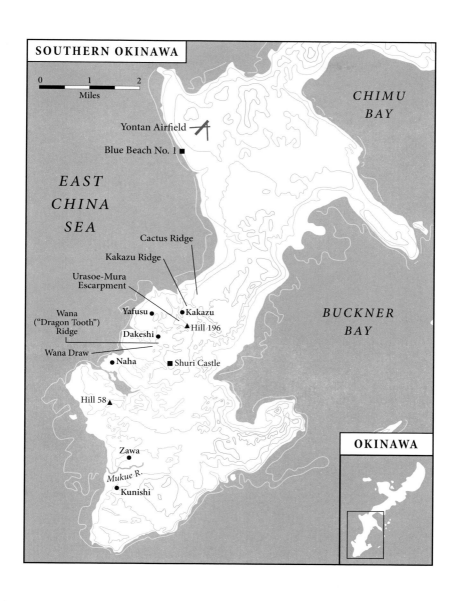

SOUTHERN OKINAWA

0   1   2
Miles

Yontan Airfield

Blue Beach No. 1 ■

CHIMU
BAY

EAST
CHINA
SEA

Cactus Ridge

Kakazu Ridge

Urasoe-Mura
Escarpment

Wana
("Dragon Tooth")
Ridge

Yafusu ●

● Kakazu

▲ Hill 196

BUCKNER
BAY

Dakeshi ●

Wana Draw

● Naha

■ Shuri Castle

Hill 58 ▲

Zawa
●

Mukue R.

● Kunishi

OKINAWA

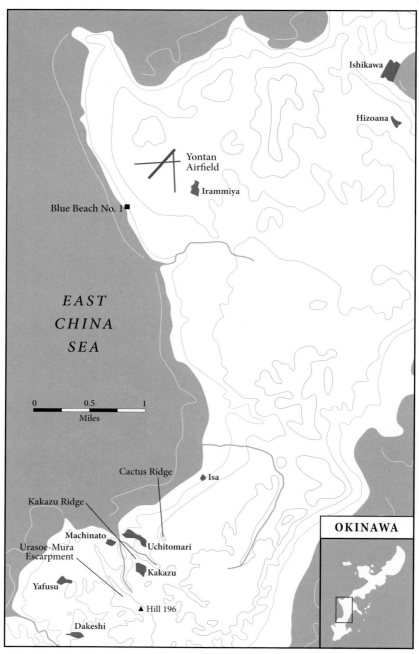

Area traversed by Donner's section from April 1, 1945, to April 29, 1945.

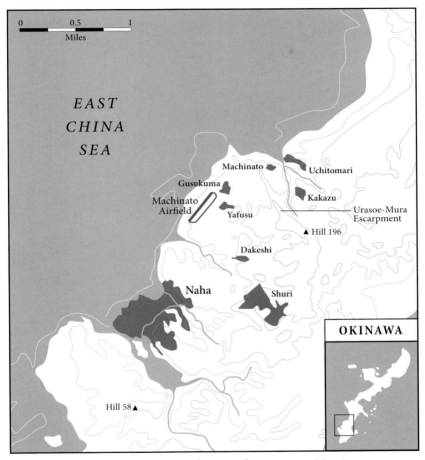

Area traversed by Donner's section from April 29, 1945, to May 6, 1945.

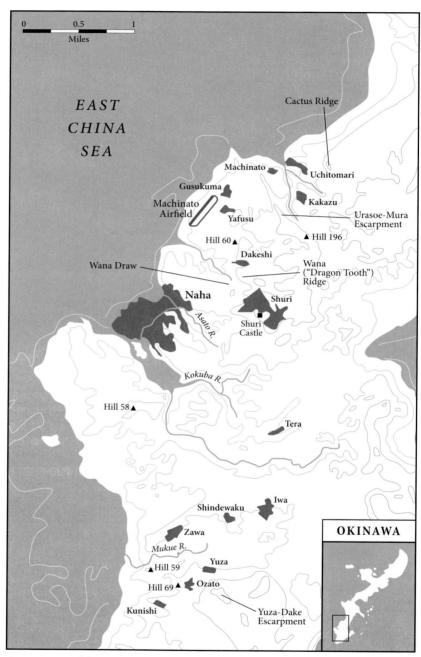

Area traversed by Donner's section from May 6, 1945, to July 1, 1945.

stuck tank, and came along beside the left of the knoll. Men were kneeling at the ready, hesitating before pushing ahead. All of a sudden, there was a sound from the brush. Knee mortar shells went almost straight up into the air from some hidden caves. Then they started their descent, and I saw one headed for me. Like a man in a dream, I ran from beneath it, trying to keep it in sight. At the last moment, I dove for the deck and flattened out. I heard its seemingly feeble "pop," and heard a man near me swear. He called out for a hand. I went over to him and saw that a jagged tear had been ripped above his boot. He put an arm around my shoulders, and I helped him back to the OP, where a corpsman took over.

Returning to my scouting now, I passed the brushy knoll and moved along a path which skirted the top of a cliff overlooking a valley. A hundred yards beyond the knoll was a tank with a handful of soldiers crouching beside the motionless vehicle. I caught up to them and asked who was ahead. "No one," was their answer.

"Where are you headed?" I wanted to know.

A sergeant pointed across a field along a prolongation of the cliff edge.

"Then let's get there," I remarked as matter-of-factly as I could. "I need an OP."

I walked into the field, feeling absurdly exhilarated, as if I were taking a ride on a roller-coaster. Four or five men followed me, two others staying with the tank. The latter shouted that the tank would not advance. The men hesitated, looking at one another. I walked on, and they ran back to the tank, which was partially concealed from the front by several high bushes. I felt that I'd be damned if I'd turn back. Then I remembered Fullmer and the sniper's bullet. I crouched low in a slight depression. From there, I could overlook the valley and the hills to the front. It would make an ideal OP. I rose and rushed back. More soldiers had reached the tank, and I could see they were preparing to occupy the area I had just crossed.

When I reached my OP, a naval officer was talking to Sorenson. He wanted to know where to establish an OP for naval gunfire. I told him where I had been and where I intended moving as soon as the company had established a line. Then, figuring I should inform the Exec of my intended move, I crossed the saddle and onto the right of the bushy knoll. There was a burst of Nambu fire very close at hand. Ten yards away from me, on the side of the knoll, a soldier, who had been bending over the mouth of a cave, fell backward violently. I ran to him, as did two others. The boy sat up and blinked. I felt sick, for his entire chin had been shot away and the colored organs of his throat showed as clearly as they would on a decapitated chicken. There was little blood. He sat stunned but conscious, and I don't know if he realized then. One of his buddies yelled for a medic. I ran for our corpsman and brought him up. The poor kid looked at the wound and began to weep. I know he was scared to touch it, but he began to put on the bandages as I moved on to find the Exec.

I found him behind a small bank and Captain Sweet with him. Before I had time to talk, an artillery barrage sent me diving behind the bank. The barrage lasted fifteen minutes and seemed widespread. Then came sounds of machine-gun firing up front. In a few moments, reports came over the company wire that the front line, along the cliff edge, was pinned down by intense sniping from across the valley. I returned to the OP, my plans of advance curtailed. I fired at a possible target on the far left.

Behind us, at the base of the hill, was a staff car. A party ascended the hill, clad in neat-looking dungarees but without insignia. I recognized Lt. Gen. Simon Bolivar Buckner, the Tenth Army's commander. He and another older officer took the foxhole next to mine. They were there a few minutes, looking over the front on the sunny afternoon, when a mortar barrage of yellow and pink smoke fell all about the hill. The generals and everyone else ducked. Then the brass departed hurriedly.

Within five minutes, a terrific barrage of heavy artillery began to hit the top of the hill. After the first two salvos had landed to the rear and left of us, all the other personnel took off down the right rear. I moved about twenty yards back of the summit with the radiomen, falling into a deep foxhole as the next salvo hit. All hell seemed to break loose, and I felt myself pounded up and down in the hole. The roar drowned my senses. Two big ones hit, one on either side, so that I was blown out to the side and covered with dirt and rocks. My heart was really chattering. And then the shelling moved forward and ceased. I was thankful to be alive, rose on rubbery knees, and began to look around for my team, who I was sure would be dead. Deep craters were all about us. But, one by one, the boys stood up and grinned. The poor corpsman was badly shaken. He asked to be allowed to go back to Battalion. I gave him permission, but told him that I didn't think he had a concussion. He stayed on and felt better later.

Our radio was out of commission and our wire cut. None of the Army would go back on the hill, and I didn't want to risk our own hides up there any longer. The cliff edge had proved too hot for the soldiers, who had evacuated a number of wounded on the run, and who now occupied a line following a low bank across the fields to the right of Hill 58. We joined them there, digging in for the night and realizing that we could not restore our communications before morning.

It was already dark when we had our holes dug at the right side of the saddle. I was called over to talk to the captain, who had a small cave in a mound near the center of the field. It was pitch black as I started back. I tried to walk quietly from foxhole to foxhole of the front line, but after about fifty yards, I lost one and stumbled over the rough field, not knowing where I was. After going straight ahead for perhaps thirty yards, I heard a challenge in English: "Halt! Who goes there?"

I couldn't think of the password and just stood rooted to the spot. If it had been a Marine outfit, I would have been fired upon in that pause, if not before the challenge. I called out that I was the artillery FO. "Well, get the hell back here where you won't be shot," was the kind answer. I made for the sound of the voices and stumbled past two boys gripping rifles. I thanked them briefly and inwardly blessed them.

Artillery fire was heavy that night, though most of it landed in the field behind us. Just at dawn came a barrage, one round of which threw dirt into my foxhole and half covered my carbine.

I was just sitting with the men, eating a ration for breakfast on this morning of May 1, when I heard shouts from the infantry. I jumped up and saw a Jap running from the very cave at which the man had his jaw shot off. I grabbed my carbine, took easy aim at about one hundred yards, and squeezed. The damn carbine, full of dirt from the shelling, jammed. As I cleared the chamber, two of the infantrymen fired. The Jap fell and rolled. Then he was up, hobbling and dragging a shattered leg as fast as he could through some bushes to the edge of the cliff. I got off a round just as he disappeared from sight into the valley.

As soon as we restored our wire, there was news from FDC that the First Division was coming in to relieve the Twenty-seventh that very afternoon. Another FO team would arrive to replace us.

I spent the morning back on the hill with an Army FO, firing at various targets across the valley. Meanwhile, the company managed to move up to the cliff edge with only slight sniper opposition. By afternoon, however, Hill 58 was again untenable because of Jap artillery, whose source I reported as beyond Shuri, and the cliff line was under machine-gun and mortar fire.

By 2:00 P.M., a reconnaissance group of Marines, including the company commander who was to relieve Sweet, arrived on the scene. Sweet had just been telling me that when the weak 105th Regiment had broken and run before the great Jap counterattack on Saipan, his unit of the 106th had been the first to be called up from reserve to stem the Nips, who were using pitchforks, sabers, and anything handy in their suicidal last try. And now, that same 105th was again bogged down on our left.

The Marine captain wished to be shown the lines. When Sweet warned him that it might be better to form a line where we had been the previous night, the "Leatherneck" drew himself up and said, "I have been ordered to take over your positions, and I won't give an inch." Then he stated that his company of 240 would do the job of the two Army companies. Sweet replied that those two Army companies had been doing the job with less than two hundred men between them.

They went on their reconnaissance and returned in thirty minutes. The Marine CO had his arm in a sling, having been hit by a sniper. He went to a hospital. It was so damn funny that, for once, I had to laugh with the Army, as did my whole FO team.

The Marines came in under the direction of their exec, who rushed hither and yon, doing an effective job of placing them. At times, the bursts of machine-gun fire told us that the action was observed. It required almost two hours just to replace the soldiers, at the end of which initial period there were already six Marine casualties, more than that company had sustained in its entire first month on Okinawa.

About 5:00 P.M., one of my men told me that the new Marine captain had arrived. I walked over the saddle and continued along the bank until I reached our other FO team. There was a Marine captain with them. He saw me, grinned broadly, and said, "Hello, Chris." Looking under his helmet, I finally recognized the rosy cheeks of Hennessey, who had flown with Sigler and me from Honolulu. I said, "How is it that you're with this infantry company?" Hennessey told me that he had been with regimental weapons in command of M-7s until today. Then, with the regular CO hospitalized, he had been quickly transferred. I told him that I thought it was something hot to receive his first infantry command in the lines, in a hot spot, and not knowing anyone in the company. He laughed heartily and asked if we were his artillery support. I said that we were until our relief arrived. It was obviously too late to pull out that night, although the men were unhappy that they couldn't return to the Battalion.

In the morning, after having fired several missions from the left OP at likely Jap positions, I joined the men in entering some of the Jap tunnels that honeycombed Hill 58 and must have run down into the valley before they were wrecked. That hill had earlier been a Jap regimental weapons headquarters. We found stocks of uniforms, clothing such as sweaters and socks, ammo, stationery, fountain pens, rubber garments, prophylactics, and machine guns. From a dead officer came a serviceable map case, which I used for the balance of the campaign because it would roll up and was light in weight. I took a sweater and socks, while the men loaded up with all they could carry. At last, the relief arrived, with a team of three, and we trudged back along the railroad tracks to the village of Gusukuma, where our battery truck picked us up.

The Battalion had by now moved its guns up the coast to a beach position just south of Machinato village. I was awfully happy to see the shelters and the mess hall with its hot chow. I even felt safe, took a bath, shaved, and slept thirteen hours after reading much mail from home.[4]

I now assumed charge of local defense for the battery. And, on the night of May 3, we were treated to a crazy show, as only the Japs knew how to put them on. Shortly after nightfall, a number of Nip bombers came in one after another, dumping their eggs in our general vicinity, but in hit-or-miss fashion that did no real harm. That was a prelude to surface action. While I sat talking to Dick Woods about making out a power of attorney for Madge, we were alerted by the Navy that a Jap landing force was headed for our beach. At once, I placed the men at our beach machine-gun posts and riflemen in several positions. Some two thousand yards away, we could see naval patrol boats firing tracers at short range. We were alert just about all night, but though some unfortunate Nips landed above and below our beach, we never saw any.

My rest period was short, and on May 6 three of us—Bob Main as liaison and Gunner Kerr and I heading FO teams—were trucked up to the bivouac area of the First Marines, just three hundred yards to the rear of Hill 58. We joined them in the afternoon because the outfit was scheduled to go into action early the next morning. This was the hilly, red-clay region through which I had approached the Twenty-seventh Division. The rain began about supper time. In an amphitheatre-like area, I dug a shallow foxhole and suspended a poncho over it.

During the night, the rain became a downpour. I was rudely awakened by the poncho giving way under a great bay of water, which soaked me and filled the hole. When I tried to reconstruct the shelter, a sentry shouted that he would shoot if he heard any further noise "over there." I told him that the Japs would do their best to be quiet. And then I lay on the ground, wrapped in the soaking wet poncho.

CHAPTER 6

May 7 to June 11, 1945

V-E Day in Europe, as war still raged near Hill 58; spotting for the
First Marines at Dakeshi, Dragon Tooth Ridge, and Wana Draw;
the fall of Naha and Shuri Castle; civilian casualties; supporting the
breakout toward Yuza, Kunishi, and the Mukue River

The morning was cold and drenching. We couldn't build a fire; the attack was postponed twenty-four hours; and we just stood and shivered. I was so wet and cold that all my skin shriveled and whitened from exposure. We tried digging a bank shelter, which crumbled on top of us. We tried a Jap cave, which was so alive with fleas that we had to get out. We found a cleaner cave and tried to burn Composition 3 to warm our clothes inside it. The C-3 just about baked us as in an oven and forced us out. We continued to be miserable. Toward noon, FDC told us by phone that the German armies had surrendered. A barrage of all artillery on the island convinced us at noon that V-E Day had arrived. We said, "Well, well, that's great." After all, it didn't change our date with the front lines on the morrow.

The rain stopped late in the afternoon. We really cheered up at that. A cold wind dried us out in unpleasant fashion. We went forward in a large group to reconnoiter in the vicinity of the railroad pass left of Hill 58.

Early morning, we moved the entire Battalion by single file to the pass, then along the right side of the railroad trestle to a couple of small sharp hills three hundred yards to the front. This was the present front line, and the three hundred yards represented the entire gain made by this fresh unit of Marines in seven days of fighting.

The infantry halted behind the hill to the left of the track. I went up to a flattened end of the hill with officers of B Company. We crouched low and looked over a narrow valley which ran from the left of the hill for five hundred yards in front of us. I was to observe the initial barrage and then fire at targets of opportunity.

By midmorning, the attack began. Several battalions of artillery blasted away as the infantry started to file out below me in the valley. Canister smoke shells were fired, but whatever outfit was using them had short dope, and the canisters fired into our own men. I saw several casualties and quickly radioed FDC to send out "cease fire" on the smoke. But it was several minutes before the missiles stopped falling on our troops.

My radioman was in a cave mouth opening upon that small flattop. I quickly joined him when several enemy mortar shells fell on my supposedly private OP. I wasn't too happy about that cave, however, because some Japs had crawled out of it the night before and knifed some of the infantry.

Now the attack gained momentum, despite muddy going. The Nambu fire was intense, and a steady stream of stretchers came back down the valley. I could see bursts of action: our men pinned down halfway up the opposite hillsides, grenades tossed into caves, Japs jumping up and running but riddled with bullets before going fifty yards. The valley was cleared within two hours. The demolition men came in with satchel charges to seal the cave entrances. I had fired at two Jap machine-gun positions as my share of helping the action.

They called me forward at this point. I met the Battalion's CO, who explained that I could find a fine observation point right at the apex of the new line. He was a young colonel and quite an eager beaver. I went to pick up my team, and as we came forward, laying wire, we passed the colonel, who was being taken out on a stretcher. He had been nicked while taking a look from our "good" OP.

Gunner Kerr, who had already reached the forward line, had not been able to decide on an OP. He was receiving little help from the First Marines, who were trying to organize a triangular defense with the apex set at a small conically shaped hill. This was right out in front of everything. Climbing to its narrow point, I found good observation to both sides of our front line. Darkness was already closing in, and I spent a busy two hours firing several problems at points from which the infantry thought it was receiving mortar and 47 mm fire, and after that in registering protective barrages with 105 mm, 75 mm (an amphtrack outfit), and 155 mm howitzers. It was all adjustment by flash and sound, but I had seen enough of the terrain at dusk to sense the bursts closely.

About 9:00 P.M., I tried to find the CO of B Company. It was then that I discovered that he and another officer had also become casualties. The acting CO, a tall, thin, dark-haired chap who looked completely bushed, had just finished the terrific job of organizing the position under fire. I remembered that I had two 2-ounce bottles of medical brandy, with which Doc Wetzell had supplied each member of the team before leaving. I gave the CO one and was almost overcome by his gratitude. It seemed to bolster his spirits immensely within a few minutes.

We scooped out very shallow trenches at the base of the OP hill, assigned watches to cover the phone on the OP, and lay down for some much-needed sleep. An hour later, I was awakened by a wireman. There was a message from FDC, asking me to observe massed fires at 11:00 P.M. I swore gently but firmly. Even before I could rise, there was a terrific whooshing overhead. The thunder and reverberations followed. I looked at my watch. It was 11:01 P.M. I sent a message back that it had sounded fine, and I was soon fast asleep.

Again in the night, I awakened. There seemed to be firing all around me. Then it stopped. Blackness and stealthy movement near at hand closed in. I took a good grip on my jungle knife and waited, and waited. I must have gone to sleep waiting.

I didn't wake until dawn. I rose and looked down the trail on which we had been sleeping. Fifty feet away on the trail, a dead Jap was sprawled. Ten feet farther on was another, slumped over a heavy machine gun. And there were four others in a short distance. All dead—all a few yards behind our front line where it left the conical hill and stretched back across the valley.

The infantry were still sleeping or sitting, two men to a foxhole. I crouched down and ran along the line until I came to a slender, blond kid who was cleaning a BAR. I asked him who got the Nips.

"I did," he answered.

"With that?" I asked, pointing at the BAR.

"Yes, sir. I was standing watch when I thought I heard a movement behind me. Figured it would be our men, but I turned anyhow. Just then, a flare lit things up and I saw their shapes and the Nambu. I opened up."

I complimented him without really being able to tell him what I thought. We were on that trail the Japs were following. They would have walked over us next. It struck me that they must have been a suicide squad.

While eating rations, I heard a shout and, looking up, saw something like an ash can come hurtling end-over-end through the air.[1] It was headed for the line of foxholes across the valley. The men rose as a group and dashed back. There was a terrific explosion as it landed. A geyser of earth shot up, and a crater thirty feet in diameter appeared. No one was hurt. The men returned to their holes. Two minutes later, as I reached the top of my OP, another came up from behind some trees six hundred yards in front. I yelled first and flattened myself, for it seemed to be overhead. The men dashed back once more. This one landed just to the right of our hill and covered everyone around with dirt, again with no casualties.

I immediately called FDC. They assigned me a 155 mm howitzer battalion for adjustment. Then there was trouble in relaying the mission over wire. An L-5 spotter plane appeared overhead. FDC informed me the plane had spotted the big mortar and would fire the mission. It was accomplished very shortly.

Bob Main, who had been serving as our liaison officer, called me back to meet him at First Battalion's headquarters. I hurried the two hundred yards to the rear. Tanks were moving up the valley, obviously in preparation for something important. Fifty yards from me, one of these M-4s rose off its tracks in a blinding flash and roar, turned completely upside down, and caught fire. Two of the tank's crew of four escaped the destruction of the land mine.

Bob now told me that I should change over to A Company, First Battalion, First Marines, and fire barrages for an attack farther up the valley. I was to coordinate my fire with that of the tanks, whose fire would be direct.

Taking the team, I made my way to a point abreast and three hundred yards to the right of our conical hill OP. I was now on the slope of Hill 60, which the Second Battalion had taken. Here, behind a low bank, was a command tank and eight others. I met the Exec of A Company and discussed with him and the tank commander the barrage they would need. Before us stretched four hundred yards of grassy field, bounded on the right by the railroad embankment and on the left by a fairly steep 150-foot cliff, spotted by caves. This high ground to the right of Dakeshi had been pummeled by all sorts of artillery in the preceding days and by my own firing on the previous morning. At the end of the field was a low rise, along which, according to the map, ran a road connecting the town of Dakeshi with the East China Sea. On this rise, I dumped the Battalion's salvos every thirty seconds for a half hour, using mixed time and demolition bursts (fuze delay). The effects appeared excellent, both on and immediately beyond the target.

Meanwhile, the tanks moved downfield, blasting away at the cliff side and at the road bed with 75s. As they approached the end of the valley, I raised the artillery fire three hundred yards to clear them as they used machine guns at close range on the remaining Japs, and as two tanks with liquid fire poured it into cave mouths.

This was a signal for the infantry. A hundred yards in front of me, a great wave of Marines sprang to their feet from the grass and moved forward, ten or fifteen feet separating each man. They blazed away in front of them with rifles and BARs. Thirty yards behind them, covering the breadth of the valley, another wave appeared, and then another. The attack was on in force, battalion in column. Up ahead, dive bombers and fighters helped prepare the way. I changed over to smoke for the artillery. Suddenly, I had the feeling that I was a kid again, sitting in a movie like "The Big Parade" and having a great thrill from a spectacle. It did thrill me. The Japs were surprised, pinned down by our firepower. They had nothing to send in return. Within thirty minutes, the road had been reached. And, on the right, the Sixth Division made a successful attack to the same line.

I immediately took my team forward to the new line, unreeling wire as fast as we could. As we reached the reverse slope of the road bed, Paul Burke, A Company's commander, met me with smiles. He was one of my classmates from ROC. Paul asked for harassing fire to the front. He thought that I might be able to locate some antitank guns that were hitting here and there along the line.

We crossed the elevated road, so worn with use by carts that its dirt surface had sunk three feet, leaving low ramparts on each side. Against the southern ramparts, the infantry advance line was crouching. I joined them, found a place that had been scooped out of the bank, and set the phone there.

I called Bob Main and began to register on a small hill three hundred yards in front. (We were now at coordinates 7774 M.2, firing at R.3.) I was just making my adjustment after the first round when I heard the crack and spat of bullets hitting human flesh and felt the air move behind my neck. I instinctively flattened against the rampart as the bullets whistled down the road just a foot or so behind me. Two Marines within ten feet of my left shoulder had crumpled. The first bullets I heard were hitting them. It was very plainly enfilade fire from a machine gun in the cliff on our left. It stopped for a moment, and three of us dove headfirst for a shallow shell hole in the roadbed. The bullets and the staccato rattle of the gun resumed as we crouched. On the phone receiver, which I couldn't reach, I could hear Main shouting my name, wanting to know what was wrong.

Farther on our right, other men were wounded. After an eternity of ten minutes, a tank took care of the machine gun. We moved out of the hole and carried the dead Marines down. I called Bob to explain, dug a better hole in the bank—although I suppose the other slight indentation had saved my life—and went on firing. The feeling of exultation had departed. Back of me, I heard shouts of "shoot the bitch, shoot the Jap woman." On top of the cliff on the left appeared an Okinawan, carrying in her arms what appeared to be a baby. She must have been allowed past our lines on that sector. There were shots. She fell. Then she struggled to her feet, moved over to pick up the baby. More shots. She went down and was still. When I could leave my post and go down behind the road, none of the men there would own up to having fired.

Within the hour, now late afternoon, Lieutenant Swanson arrived with another FO team to relieve us. The trip back through the valley was now dangerous. The Japs were covering it from high ground with indirect machine-gun fire. We had to dive for cover more than once coming back. But, despite a long trek, we were mighty happy to return to the battery, safe and sound. It was May 10.

There was a night's rest only at the battery. Then, with Dick Woods up as liaison, I had to take over the Exec's duties. On the night of the 11th, Gibson reported from his OP a counterattack in the middle of the night, upon a line two hundred yards forward of the area that I had left. Until 0400, we continued to poop out round after round, with reports coming back that the Japs were being slaughtered by the hundreds. There was the monotonous repetition of angle and quadrant settings, and then: "Check 1, check 4, check 3 . . . Number 2, are you ready, you're holding us up, Number 2. Check 2. Ready, Fire!" All this from a little canvas shack, surrounded by sandbags, figuring deflections and time. And outside, the shouts of the gunners, the breech slamming on the nearest piece, the blast of the guns with the farthest sounding late, but all flashing together in the night. Monotonous, yet feeling safe, because one knew that it was nothing like the real thing on the line to which he would have to return in two days.

There were more attempted Jap landings up the beach, and again they were broken up by naval gunfire. In the morning came reports from Gibson that 250 dead Nips had been counted in front of the Marine line where the counterattack had been staged.

On May 14, I took another FO team up by truck to a small hill on the right-hand side of the railroad and in line with the wagon road bed running to Dakeshi. Here Dick Woods briefed me on the area, explaining how the First Marines had managed to move along the right side of the railroad but had not been able to advance up the valley on the left. And the Japs still held Wana gorge in the high cliffs across the way. After Dick had shown me several concentrations, I walked the team forward following the right side of the rail embankment, which was ten feet high at this point. After fifteen minutes, we reached a small dirt road at a point where it crossed the track to the ruins of three old houses overlooking the valley. This was the position of the advance company, E Company of the Second Battalion, First Marines. As we started across the road, bullets kicked up the dust in front of us. One at a time, we covered that open space as fast as we could move with heavy equipment.

F Company adjoined E Company, with the CPs on either side of the road within conversational distance. One of the first things we were told was to get our holes quickly because the artillery fire was heavy. A three-foot bank provided the only real shelter, other than the stone foundation of the house. Most of the CP's foxholes were behind this. We occupied three empty ones and were just setting up the radio when a tank appeared from our rear, following the road. Within two minutes, there was heavy artillery fire landing all over the place. Just by chance, I was looking over at F Company's CP and saw a shell hit the bank in front of them, ricochet, and burst over their heads, all in an instant. The cries of the wounded men were pitiful: one with his stomach opened, another with a leg virtually torn off. There were two dead, one decapitated. It was sickening.

I climbed out to some bushes in front of the house and tried to figure where the enemy artillery was located. There were flashes from behind a hill, for which I sent an azimuth to FDC, but the range was indeterminable. The regiment tried all sorts of fires, but every few minutes, more shells would come over.

On our right front, units of the Twenty-ninth Regiment of the Sixth Division staged an attack. We saw them go out, heard intensive small-arms firing, and a half hour later at dusk saw them running back to form a line with us. It rained all night. I had my team sleep among the houses' foundations, keeping off the rain with ponchos. And I spent most of the night trying to find an Okinawa version of "Pistol Pete" to appease the company commander who claimed his men were demoralized by the artillery shelling. Once, after I had fired a concentration where I thought he might be, Pete was silent for an hour. I lay down, and he opened up again.

The First Marines were supposedly relieved by the Fifth Marines that night, although we did not get out before morning. Walking back through the rain and mud along the railroad, I met Captain Hennessey. His cheeks were sallow, his usually bright eyes sunken. I asked him how it was going. "It's terrific, Chris," he said. "When you left us two weeks ago, we had 240 fresh men. I lost down to ninety. They gave me seventy-five replacements a few days ago, and I'm already down to eighty. I don't see how it can go on at that rate. Thank God we're getting a rest."

From May 2 on Hill 58 to Hennessey's present position on May 15 was just 2,000 yards in two weeks, at the cost of 215 casualties out of 315. It was the last time I saw Captain Hennessey. He was shot through the head the next time he led his men into action.

At the battery again, I relaxed a bit more than usual. The Seabees had moved into the Battalion's beach area and were constructing a sandy embankment to serve as a future LCT dock. They used carryalls. I watched them and even strolled along the beach several hundred yards to find a spot suitable for swimming. I visited FDC, which was at this time in the bottom of an old quarry pit. The Battalion-2 furnished me with new maps and information about the front lines that he had never seen.

The strain of repeated trips to the front was beginning to tell quite a bit on men and officers, although the officers caught it twice as often. One's pulse beat faster and the appetite waned as the morning approached for the next job. Experience is a forceful teacher, and at no time at the front had I failed to see numbers of men killed quite near me. When, therefore, we arrived at the First Marines' bivouac on the afternoon of May 18 to find that the orders had been changed and they would not move up until the next morning, it was a bit of a relief.

But the morrow dawned, and glumly, I took a team along to join the First Marines. We moved along a back road through the increasingly steep hills toward Dakeshi. In terribly heavy fighting, the Seventh Marines—in fact, my old friends of the Second Battalion—had taken and obliterated that tiny hillside village. They were passing out of the line as we moved in, and I looked for familiar faces, but I recognized only a couple in the long files of bedraggled, sweaty figures. At last, I reached a ridge line of battered tombs overlooking the village. There among shattered trees and tumbled broken rocks, I found O'Mahoney, gaunt and bearded, bitter and uncertain. He told me it had been hell in the last few days. The day before, Captain Grass had been killed. Lieutenant Warren had died in an earlier action. Now, every headquarters officer was handling a company–what was left of them. Huff was a company commander, and Gunnigle was still sticking along with them for naval gunfire. O'Mahoney then pulled out.

The ridge was a stinking mess, compounded by half-empty ration tins, dead Japs, and human feces, all covered with hot flies. Across a green valley was another ridge, six hundred yards in front of us. On its crest, beyond which I could not see, stood an enormous rock in the shape of a tooth. On its right extremity, the ridge sloped down to the long transverse valley through which ran the railroad, and beyond which I could see the remaining buildings of the capital city of Naha. The ridge was called by the Marines "Dragon Tooth Ridge" (really Wana Ridge). On the other side of it was Wana Draw.

At the right end of the ridge, another battalion of the First Marines assaulted from the lower ground, trying to sweep up toward the Dragon's Tooth. MacDonald of our battalion was conducting the artillery barrages. I could sit in my OP (two boulders and a tree stump), listening to Mac and watching the slow progress of the infantry. All of a sudden, two tanks, which were blasting away at the side of the ridge, were hit by 47s; heavier machine-gun and mortar fire raked the men and drove them back. They managed to retain only a small section at the right-hand end of the ridge.

I fired the usual registration on the opposite ridge, moved the radio into a tomb, wrote Madge a few descriptive notes, and slept in the musty atmosphere of the pitch-black interior on a narrow stone altar step. During the night, I almost knocked over an urn containing the brittle bones of someone's ancestors. It was relatively comfortable.

In the morning, our battalion began moving across the valley bottom in front of Dakeshi and up the far slope in an attack of Wana Ridge. I accompanied company headquarters and had just about reached the small stream at the bottom, when the men halfway up on Dragon Tooth Ridge ran into a fire fight with a well-concealed enemy. There was nothing for us to do but sit behind a two-foot bank and wait. I wrote more notes to Madge, having to hug the ground once or twice, when some Jap heavy artillery crashed in volleys a hundred feet behind us. We ate rations, and later I scouted up a trail to the left, but was shot at. Not even knowing where the bullets came from, I dove into a gulley and ran back to the team.

Finally we double-timed, one man at a time, over an open slope to the forward line of the infantry, behind a terrace-like break in the hillside. It provided a very thin defensive line, but was as far as the men had been able to advance—about two hundred yards short of the summit.

This terrace arrangement had been one of my targets the day before. Now we found a few dead Japs lying around, from one of which I picked up a rifle in fair condition. The cliff contained a number of cave entrances, in our exploring of which we found three levels of tunnels and subterranean rooms, all interconnecting. We doubled our watch that night, keeping sharp lookout at the mouths of these caves.

About 9:00 P.M., I was informed by FDC over wire that my company would assault early in the morning. Wooster wanted to know if I could observe. I replied that by looking over the edge of the terrace, I could see the ridge line, but not beyond, where they wished to have the barrage. He told me that I ought to be able to hear them anyhow and advised me on the type of fire to use. I went over to the CO, who had not even heard that he was scheduled for the assault. At the same time, there was a little mortar duel going on between our men behind the terrace and the Japs on the ridge.

Early in the morning of May 21, I was just awakening in the first light, sitting up, half covered by my blanket, when I heard a rustling on the other side of the terrace over my head. (Here, it was about six feet high.) I had just grasped my carbine when a man landed on my head and shoulders, bringing down on my forehead a dislodged rock that almost knocked me cold. But I grabbed him and rolled over, only to find it was a young, smallish Marine. I'll never forget the surprised, frightened look on his face.

"Where are you headed, man?" I asked.

For answer, he only asked me where company headquarters were. I pointed to the left. Then, with an agitated "Oh!" he scuttled as fast as a monkey down into the valley and toward the right. He carried no pack or rifle. I believe I had seen my only Marine deserter in combat.

Within a few moments, I was firing the barrage over the ridge. The company did not attack at once, and I had to repeat some of the fire, which may or may not have done any good. This time, the boys made good their dash for the top, where mortar fire hit them on arrival, causing them to think some of our artillery was falling short.

Unfortunately, the Army's Seventy-seventh Division, on the left, lagged in their attack, with the result that sniper fire from the left was intensive upon the rear of our new front line. The mortars continued to pop all over the place. One corporal was dragged back and given a transfusion. His foot was gone at the ankle. When they could bring up a stretcher and start off with the man, he began to smoke a cigarette someone had given him. Then, with his face drawn with pain, he waved to us and shouted, "Got mine, fellows. Gonna have liberty now. Good luck to you."

The stretcher-bearers were busy all morning. A Jap came out of a tunnel through the ridge and opened up with a machine gun on the backs of our front lines. A combat squad finished him, but not until after he had scored.

Before midmorning, Walter Burke, the new company CO, called back for us. Those two hundred yards to the ridge line were under almost steady fire. It was tough with the radio, but we made it, running in short dashes from shell hole to shell hole, until we reached a tomb. I stuck the radio and operator in the tomb, crawled over the bodies of two dead Marines, and on my belly edged up the last ten feet of almost pulverized rock to the skyline. A Marine was lying in a shallow foxhole up there, rifle at the ready. But he couldn't see forward into Wana Draw because of some jagged rock masses a few feet in front of him. I knew I must see past those if I wanted good observation. Still on my belly, I wriggled past him, over the narrow crest, and among the rocks. I was within two feet of a dead Jap's face that peered up from a standing foxhole where he had been bayoneted.

The ridge dropped off perpendicularly for twenty-five feet to the slope of the draw, and just as I looked over, I saw four Japs, one a woman, dive into a cave mouth just below me. I signaled to the infantryman, who crept up and threw over a few grenades.

Now, I could look unobstructedly at the mass of rock and rubble which had been the fourteenth-century Shuri Castle. On the right, I could see down into Naha. But the view didn't last long. Snipers on our unprotected left flank, where the Seventy-seventh Division had not yet pulled even, were picking us up. And a barrage of Jap mortar shells began landing all along the ridge. The other Marine and I were covered with dirt from two close ones and moved down to the tomb.

My radioman meanwhile was having his troubles. Somewhere close, the Nips had a radio with which they were able to cut in on our frequency. They jabbered a great deal. We reported it to FDC, but they couldn't do anything about it. I couldn't keep wire communication because every time my men strung it, the tanks coming through the valley behind us chewed it up.

By early afternoon, the sniper fire had been cut down somewhat and the radio cleared. I tried the ridge line again and dug a shallow hole, after which I registered on Shuri. I hadn't been doing this very long before some fellow in khaki crept up by me, carrying a Graflex camera; he was a news cameraman. He borrowed my trench to take some pictures of Shuri, standing up to get some better ones of Wana Draw. A few mortar bursts nearly made him duck.

I fired one or two concentrations after that but couldn't see any definite enemy activity. To hit the cave mouths on the opposite bank of the draw, we needed high-angle fire, and the effect was nil. The ravine curved back to my right so that I couldn't see whatever was firing flat-trajectory, high velocity shells in our direction, but I could hear the business.

Soon Burke called me back to the CP. He said his men had had to fall back from their position on the ridgeline because a couple of Jap 4.7-inch guns[2] were knocking hell out of the forward crest. Could I try to put the bastards out of action? A corporal took me up to the right flank of the company where I found the men crouched along the tomb line or ten feet below the horizon. I could feel and hear the repeated explosion of shells on the other side.

I felt rather dubious of my own ability to deal with these 4.7s, but I knew I had to impress the bunch of infantry watching that the artillery could be dependable. I merely walked up the ridge and took a quick look over, turned, and walked down again. I had seen two of our own tanks: one was blasting the caves beneath us, and the other was burning them out with fire. (I thought of the three Japs and the girl who had ducked in beneath my own foxhole.) The infantrymen were relieved to hear what was doing the shooting, and Burke had little to say.

When I returned to my radiomen, I discovered that another FO team was on the way. Gibson brought them up, and we happily moved out of the shadow of the "Dragon Tooth" just as a light rain began falling. The air was clear, and I could view this horribly shattered hillside with scarcely a tree left upright and the very rocks crushed to rubble. The toll in American lives to cross this valley of a few hundred yards had been enormous. My men were terribly jittery and glad to get out.

On the opposite side of Dakeshi, I climbed a steep hill to take leave of Bill Miller, who was on liaison duty, but able to fire concentrations by smoke-spotting. His perch was under constant sniper fire. It was raining hard.

Williams and his team joined us and we headed back to the trucks, I with the Jap rifle that I had picked up on the terrace. I was thinking of

Gibson's comment when he told us that the general had commended us for the attack: "That means the old son-of-a-bitch wants us to push some more."

For the next two weeks, we battled rain and mud in unending quantities. Our shack, which had been dug into the beachfront, was swamped, with our precious cots floating about as I awoke the morning of May 26, ass-deep in water. Nothing remained dry.

From the front lines came news of a stalemate. Gibson reported that mortar fire had intensified; that he had given my foxhole to a rifleman, who had been killed in it by a sniper the morning after I left; that he had moved his team to a stronger tomb further back and had tried to keep dry.

Colonel Roe notified me that I would probably become the Battalion survey officer because of my seniority and long FO service. He sent me almost to Naha to run a base line with Swanson to a new battery position—of all places, right where I had taken Sigler's spot with the Twenty-seventh. That we should move the battery seemed almost incredible but necessary, since we were firing extreme range.

We almost had to dredge our way into the new position, for it had already rained six days. Naha had fallen on the 28th, and with clear weather on the 29th, we shoved forward. I was up helping to get the guns and the galley in place when I heard a roar of motors overhead. I noticed some of our own carrier planes coming very low. Then, suddenly, there was the swish of rockets, and several exploded just in front of our guns. I dove toward one hole, saw the water in it, and fell back into another also filled with water. Off to the left, a truck with eight men in it was hit and overturned with casualties. Later, the Navy explained that planes from the USS *Bunker Hill* had mistaken our end of the island for the Jap end. They had ranged all along our lines with blazing guns. At our old battery position, they dropped bombs on the remaining personnel. Landing craft had been gunned by these unobservant pilots.

But, on the night of the 29th, the Japs appeared to have pulled out of Shuri. By now, we had flanked that stronghold by taking Naha, and the Army, having taken Yonbaru on the east coast, was cutting in on the left. Withdrawal movements by the Japs were reportedly widespread by May 30. We were firing missions by aerial observation on retreating troops on May 31.

Just behind us in bivouac was the First Battalion, Seventh Marines. I took the first opportunity that I had to look up some of those I knew in the outfit. Here was a chance, I thought, to ask Duplantis about the fountain pen I had loaned him before we left the Russells. I found Roger Golden. He told me. Duplantis had led his men up a hillside a few weeks before. He had looked over the top and caught one in the head.

This latest death of a friend went deep. I remembered his telling me how, after Peleliu, he had been granted a thirty-day leave stateside; he had his bag packed and was waiting at the airfield when the general recalled all leaves. He had missed seeing his family for the first time in four years by a margin of a day. I remembered his good humor and helpfulness during Officer Candidates' Class. And I became anxious to finish this job against the Japs.

It rained, and the mud was so thick that every short walk was a precarious, effortful task. The labors of handling ammunition were Herculean. Trucks could scarcely move. Jeeps were useless on the roads, with some actually disappearing completely in the fluid mud holes. Only vehicles carrying food, water, or ammo were allowed toward the front lines, and later ammo, food, and water were flown over. The engineers did their best, but the rain was too much for them. Beside our position, a 155 mm howitzer battalion occupied my old Hill 58. Even now, they had trouble with a few Japs still holding out in the tunnels. We heard the shooting.

Even with all the mud, the front was moving forward rapidly. The colonel was ordered to pick a new position because we would soon be out of range. I went up with him on reconnaissance by motor. To hear him talk about it, you might think we were going to go in advance of the infantry. Actually, we chose a strip of rolling, muddy countryside across the Asato-gawa and midway between Naha and Shuri. The infantry were already two thousand yards further south. There were several small farmhouses together in what looked as if it had been a local jail. The colonel took the jail as Battalion Headquarters. While inside one of the partially destroyed houses, I heard loud, distressed crying from below. Going outside to investigate, I found a nanny goat prone beneath the collapsed timbers of the dwelling. I tried to free the poor creature but found that its neck was broken, and I put it out of misery with a couple of shots from my carbine. Then I found two white kids, barely large enough to forage for themselves. We returned to the Battalion after being tangled in terrific traffic, confused by Marine tank columns.

On June 3, amid a downpour of rain, we moved the Battalion. Each vehicle and gun had to be winched up the short, steep hills by tractor. Mud was hip deep, and everyone was drenched. The roads resembled yellow rivers. It took us six hours to travel a round trip of about four miles.

Dick Woods was on liaison duty, and I, as Battery Exec, had the pleasure of positioning our guns in the new swampland and of putting them into action. Even at that, we were the only battery ready to fire by nightfall. We slept in water, grateful of the chance to sleep at all. We fired most of the next morning, having great difficulty in keeping the pieces accurately laid because of the soft ground.

In the afternoon, I took a walk down to the front of our position on the rumor that some Okinawans were hiding out in that area. I caught sight of a little old fellow disappearing like a gnome into a cave some four hundred yards away from our position. When I reached that point, another object—as tragic as one could see—met my view. On the ground lay the body of a young Okinawan, a girl who had been fifteen or sixteen, and probably very pretty in body and face. She was nude, lying on her back with arms outstretched and knees drawn up, but spread apart. The poor girl had been shot through the left breast and had evidently been violently raped. With actual physical sickness upon me, I returned to the guns.

For two more days, Johnny and I took turns "Exec'ing" the battery. The weather dried out on June 6, and some fair chow was brought up. On the morning of the 7th, we heard that all was not going well with the FOs on the line. Johnny and I were ordered to take teams to the front. There was also word that we would find the Japs well dug-in at their last major fortified line. It left my stomach somewhat cold, for I was now anxious to last out the closing phases of this campaign and go stateside.

We left by truck that noon, circled toward the west coast and came in through Naha. A few walls and an occasional concrete building, such as a church, were left standing in that devastated capital city. It had been virtually demolished by bombs and shells.

The road led southeastward out of Naha along the shores of the Naha-Ko and banks of the Kokuba River. We heard firing from the Oroku Peninsula, where the Sixth Division was just cleaning out the Japanese naval guards. The small railroad line bordered the road and was littered with wrecked, miniature equipment. Then, we traveled due south, cutting through high hills in which were great caches of supplies, with evidence of the slaughter of Japs in retreat. Many pieces of silenced Jap artillery lined the highway. This road led through Tomusu to Iwa. On the way, we dropped Lieutenant Hennessey off to join the First Battalion, First Marines, then in reserve.

At Iwa, we should have made contact with a runner from Dick Woods, then our liaison with the Second Battalion. Our rendezvous was the intersection of railroad and highway. There was no runner, we couldn't reach Dick by radio, and shells from some enemy 150s began to fall in that vicinity. We were able to speak to FDC, however, who told us to bed down for the night and await orders.

The Army—Seventy-seventh Division MPs in this area—seemed to be evacuating many aged and decrepit civilians, riding them in jeeps to the railroad station, from which they were carted out on trucks. Reconnoitering for a protected camping spot for our men, I rode with an old couple and an MP to the reverse slope of a prominent hill to the left of the station. There, I found an Army heavy mortar outfit, whose CO was most hospitable. When I had brought our teams over, he gave us excellent new 10-in-1 rations. We dug in alongside the mortar men and were bothered by only a few long shots into the front of the position.

In early morning, we were in touch with Woods, and by 0900 were on the trail through the hills into Shindewaku, where we discovered Dick Woods at the CP of the Second Battalion. He had been doing a lot of firing from a well-placed OP, which was, however, rather far back of the lines. But then, Dick wouldn't trust Michevich—who was really a shot if he wanted to be—and Michevich was supposed to be concentrating now on souvenirs.

Johnny and I were sent forward, he to the company on the right and I to the one on the left. I found Burke and Cavanaugh in command of mine, the latter now an Exec. They occupied a pleasant hill to the right front of Shindewaku, in country which had been little affected by the war.

I immediately relieved Michevich, who showed me a tremendous roll of Japanese money and several jade works of art, together with a remarkable book by a Jap marine biologist. Mich meanwhile grumbled about our slowness and passed on the word that one of our Battalion FOs had that morning called for registration, which had fallen short and killed an NCO in Burke's company.

Burke and I went to the hilltop from which I could look across the mud-bound Iwa-Yuza road to the impressive escarpment of Yuza-Dake. Into the precipitous cliffs of the land mass, carrier planes were pouring rockets and firing cannon. The noise of this strike echoed in a terrific din across the valley. When the planes were through, heavy artillery poured great barrages against the Jap fortifications, which the Army was preparing to assault. Off to our right front were the villages of Yuza, Ozato, and Kunishi, all on high ground in the advance of the Marines and affording the Nips a strong line of final resistance. Against these we directed our artillery. One of my men running wire through some houses to the rear found a bottle of sake which he brought to me and which we gratefully shared.

An Okinawan family, one of greater culture, I believe, than the average soil diggers, gave themselves up to the company CP. The father was very dignified as he presented himself before Burke and Cavanaugh. The mother was slender, with fine features, and hair well brushed. She curtsied and persistently nudged her young son, who bewilderedly bowed each time in true dancing-school style. We all looked at each other; muttered in our own languages, which were not mutually understood; and the father accepted a cigarette from a sense of politeness, although he obviously didn't know how to smoke it. As they were directed toward Battalion, mother and father grasped junior by either arm and almost bore him along between them. A little later, another middle-aged couple emerged from hiding and approached us, he bowing and she carrying a tremendous bundle on her head. East and West again clashed. The Marines shouted for the man to help her with the burden, and one soldier even tried to effect a transfer, but the woman clung tenaciously to her possession.

Next, a ten-year-old girl who could speak English appeared. She said she knew of a cave in which many Okinawans were waiting to surrender themselves. Burke sent some men along, and she led out about sixty civilians from one hole in the hillside.

As evening came on, the Nips threw mortar fire at us and two or three well concealed 47s barked off and on at our positions. Battalion called on me to observe the massed fire of ten battalions on Yuza. Over a hundred shells landed simultaneously at 9:00 P.M. What fireworks, illuminating the valley and roaring on as each gun poured in five rounds at rapid fire. Some shots fell short, but the effect of that surprise volley on the area must have devastated everything.

Because of the mud and rapidity of movement of the front lines, water and supplies were scarce. Flights of TBFs had come over in the late afternoon of June 9 and made drops of rations by parachute. We were even using water accumulated in shell holes, adding plenty of halogen pills.[3] A pall of mosquitoes and flies hung over the lines, despite the activity of DC-3s (C-47s) spreading DDT across the countryside.

I woke early in the morning of June 9 with a headache. As the day proceeded, I sickened. The outfit began moving up in single file, passing behind the ridge from Shindewaku to the town of Zawa, about 1,500 yards southwest. We trudged through the narrow, stone-walled streets of the town, entranced by some of the attractive gardens we saw there. Most of the houses were, unfortunately, rubble. On the southern end of the community was a school building and a wide-open field, traversed by a road running south across the Mukue River. Our lines were then occupying low hills overlooking the Mukue. We crossed the field in small groups, crowding the line of the hills. The companies of the Second Battalion, now small, were mixed. I found Williams and his team dug in at this point. In fact, we were all told to sit down and wait.

Johnny showed me the concentrations he had fired over toward Tera and Kunishi. On our left front, another infantry battalion tried to push forward in company strength to some higher ground near Yuza. We could see them almost reach the top, receive heavy Nambu and mortar fire, and withdraw. An attack by our right flank elements straightened the line.

It was obvious, however, by late afternoon that we were there for the night. The bridge which carried the road over the Mukue was still in, but a patrol we sent out was pinned down by small arms fire, while reconnoitering the bridge. A 47 mm gun began blasting our positions toward nightfall. With that whanging, high-velocity sound and high-pitched whistle, it would bank shells into the hillside in front or just clear the top to land one hundred yards back in the field. Johnny and I did not stick our heads up too high at the OP, while we tried for hours to catch the muzzle-blast or some sign of where the piece might be. Sometimes we fired a concentration, and the 47 would shut up for an hour. We would just start to congratulate ourselves, when again he would open up. Every time he did, Burke would scream for us to finish him, but Burke couldn't point him out, either. I recalled the duel with "Pistol Pete" on Kolombangara almost two years before. (A long war.)

Johnny and I had the "trots," which became worse during the night, accentuated by severe stomach cramps. On the next day we took turns at the OP and in trying to evacuate where we wouldn't be hit by the 47 or by mortars. The company that Johnny was with crossed the Mukue by fording and, with limited sniper action, occupied a rugged hill to our left front. Machine-gun fire appeared to be coming from a house to the right front, and Johnny and I took turns making a precision adjustment with one piece. After about twelve adjustments we fired for effect, bracketed the house, and saw dust rise from its interior. But it still stood after we had expended a lot of costly ammo. About this time, a couple of our own machine gunners set up near us, fired a few bursts of incendiary bullets, and the whole damn house went up in flames. When we had laughed that off, I fired a beautiful timed fire problem on a ridge area near Kunishi where we thought we had spotted the 47. Half an hour later I was feeling still more futile when Pete opened up again and knocked out our wires to FDC.

Ganz went out to repair the phone lines and was hit by a small fragment of another 47. He was not incapacitated and continued his efforts. The only heavy artillery around at this time that made us uncomfortable was some of our own naval gunfire, which fell very short and made everyone nervous until it could be identified and corrected.

Civilians continued to filter through the lines and across the Mukue. One old fellow, who had been found in a cave, was carried in on a stretcher. Our corpsman was called up because the man's leg had been crushed some days before, and gangrene had infected the limb from foot to thigh. The corpsman said the fellow didn't have a chance and recommended an overdose of morphine instead of risking two bearers on the long, dangerous carry back to an aid station. In his statement, the corpsman referred to the oriental as a Jap. At that point, we discovered that the old boy spoke English, for he protested loudly that he was a real Okinawan, that he hated Japs, loved Americans, and begged that we spare his life. I broke in on the discussion to tell Burke that I thought we must get the man to an aid station, no matter what he was. The civilian was delirious before he was carried off.

Night again, and Johnny and I figured we could pick up the flash of the 47 mm gun. We decided it must be pushed out of a cave to fire and then pulled back after a few rounds. Therefore, we fixed a concentration with FDC and stood ready to call for it the moment the 47 might flash. About 2200, a shell came over, and Johnny called FDC. Someone was adjusting a normal barrage for the night. Johnny screamed to clear the wire and hold up the barrage for our target of opportunity, but FDC paid us no heed. Dick Woods, taking it all in as our liaison, was furious. Meanwhile, Pete flashed at will and finally quit, though it was forty-five minutes before we could clear communications. There wasn't another chance at Pete that night, and I was so sick at both ends that I didn't care.

On the morning of the 11th, we received word that our company would cross the Mukue, use the 59-meter hill captured the day before as a line of departure, and take the 69-meter hill between Ozato and Tera. As we were eating rations—I felt too awful to try more than crackers—an infantryman who also had the trots, according to his buddies, stepped out of his foxhole and stopped to relieve himself. A sniper caught him in the head.

Lt. Bob Groshon appeared on the scene at this point to confer with Burke. Bob had a unit of our M-7 weapons carriers for support of the attack. It was decided to move them out of Zawa along our road and across the Mukue bridge. As the vehicles rumbled down the way at fifty-yard intervals, approaching the cut in the hill line which overlooked the bridge, old "Pistol Pete" awoke with a vengeance. He was over on his first round but with short range and flat trajectory blasted the first M-7. The others tried to disperse, but the fields around the second were just ooze. It bogged down, and being hit after a few more rounds, burst into flame. The crew had escaped when the vehicle mired. Johnny and I fired our concentration, but the 47 had probably quit anyhow by the time our shells landed. The other two M-7s pushed across the bridge.

The infantry now filed down to the Mukue, crossed on footbridges, and climbed the reverse slope of Hill 59. We went along, working hard to lug the heavy radio parts on the steep trail in intense heat. But as our part of the column tried to move around the right end of the hill, a stream of machine-gun bullets sprayed the path a few feet in front of us. We dove for cover just as another burst kicked up the dust where we would have been. Bullets ricocheted wildly among the rocks, and the firing was maintained on the path area for twenty minutes or so before we could move on.

We made our way forward now with company headquarters to the front of Hill 59 and could see the infantry working their way by fire teams up the slope of the next high ground. Even though they ran forward from a broader front, they seemed to converge to any terrain feature, such as a gully, that afforded cover. Then, mortar shells would drop on that particular spot and make things uncomfortable. Bearers began to carry back several wounded. They said the rifle fire was hell up on the slope and that the attack had stalled short of the top.

We moved with headquarters off Hill 59 to a point at which the road from our rear met a railroad spur coming from behind Hill 59. Heavy mortar fire made us take cover behind the railroad embankment. The entire action was becoming static. I had the men contact FDC on the radio. We were told that Gibson and Michevich should be at Hill 59 at any moment to effectuate our relief. The infantry couldn't use us where we were, and all barrages for the attack had been conducted from early morning by Battalion liaison. So I took the team back to Hill 59 and was relieved about noon. We hurried through the fields, skirted Zawa, and found Williams and his team waiting for us in a truck.

Though I did not realize it at the time, I had seen my last large-scale action.

CHAPTER 7

June 11 to August 14, 1945

War's end: the last days of the campaign; farewells to the Eleventh Marines; sailing home on the aircraft carrier USS Card

As Battery Exec for the next few days, I fired from a semirecumbent position, having little reserve after four days of "trots." On June 14, the Battalion displaced forward to a position in sugar cane fields just back of Zawa. Our principal activity now was that of stopping Jap soldiers who were trying to escape from the pocket in the south by coming through our lines. Acting as Exec in charge of the battery's security, I established gun posts and spent most of the nights on the telephone. Our battery killed at least four the first night in the position, and several more each night for the next five nights. The Nips would not allow themselves to be taken prisoner, using grenades and revolvers against our automatic weapons. We had no casualties. Tremendous numbers of civilians gave themselves up. Old women emerged from three weeks' concealment beneath flattened houses in Zawa. General Buckner was killed in the front lines.[1]

Units of the Eighth Marines of the Second Division relieved the Seventh Marines and took over our artillery missions. Huff and Gunnigle, both looking like the wrath of God, dropped in to see me and enjoyed their first galley-cooked meal in a month. Huff had become a company commander, one of the few officers in his battalion to escape being hit. They summarized the fate of the company with which I had come ashore. Only ten men had escaped being casualties. Mason, Warren, and two officer replacements had been killed. O'Mahoney, Janick, and Smith received serious wounds that caused their evacuation from Okinawa.

We now had a pool betting on the final day of the campaign. Williams won the $25 stake when the last Japanese resistance surrendered on June 21 at 4:00 P.M. There were immediately a lot more smiles and light remarks going about than I had seen for some time. A naval officer friend of Miller donated a side of beef to the battery from the ship's locker, and we dined on fresh meat for the first time in two months. Four other officers and I, having had a small drink from a bottle just out of the States and a cigar apiece, took our jeep bounding over a beat-up mountain road toward Iwa to a motor transport outfit in the rear which was showing a movie, "Song of the Open Road." The entertainment was at least amusing, and our good spirits there in the large garden of an old house made it an occasion. The ride back through burnt-out villages, across wide areas without visible humans, and our way so illuminated by star shells that we did not use headlights, was really weird. Machine guns and sniper rifles were constantly firing nervously, and we had our carbines ready for any suspicious activity along the deserted roadside or in the wreckage of villages because our painfully slow speed made us a good target for a grenade. It was a swell evening. We occupied that position until the end of June, playing volleyball and catching up on sleep and food.

About the first of July, I moved with the advance echelon of the Battalion far north on Okinawa to a point on the northwestern shore of Motobu Peninsula. Here, the entire First Division was to encamp, rest, and reorganize. The countryside was clean, open, pine-wooded, and really attractive, though too hot for comfort at this season. The land rose steeply in coral cliffs to a ridge, then sloped gradually through a broad, fertile plain to rather steep mountains. In the next month, we were busily building a hurricane-proof camp of "strongbacked" tents.

Our minds were concentrated, above all else, on the question of home. This was an outfit with long duty overseas. How many could expect replacements, how soon? All sorts of theories were rife, and rumors, "straight dope," began to run freely. When would the release of troops from fighting in Europe affect the part played by the Army out here? Would we leave on a point system? The next campaign must be Kyushu. Would we have to be back for it, if we went stateside? So it went.

And, with the cessation of fighting, our rear echelon gear caught up with us calling for labor details. It also meant beer for the men and liquor for the officers. Drinking and cards became the order of the night, and with these, one heard far more talk about the girls at home. I thought more of Madge and wrote longer letters concerned with getting home. Some officers began to find excuses for taking a jeep down the island. They were looking for liquor and nurses but found little of either.

I found, too, that I wanted quiet and solitude, so I began to make frequent strolls through the pleasant streets of the village behind our camp. The homes were intact but deserted because the natives had been removed to a general compound across the peninsula. I also went bathing every day and discovered a beautiful coral grotto with a half-submerged, small entrance but with a main chamber fully twenty feet high, hung with stalactites and stalagmites.

When I had completed a week of unloading details, I was assigned by Colonel Roe to directing coral surfacing on the camp roads. Then I had to direct the building of the COs' tents and finally was put in charge of designing and building the officers' mess hall, calculated to be an elaborate club on the ridge overlooking sea and camp. Progress was not rapid. We felt lazy, and the intense heat made us lazier. I went to movie after movie for two weeks and then lost interest. It seemed to me that the sound was never satisfactory, that it couldn't be heard clearly. Then, I developed an itching in the ear and was treated for fungus.

At last, in the middle of July, a list came out; those officers and men whose names appeared on the list were in line for early return to the States. Mine wasn't on the list. I was two months shy of the thirty-month minimum. Two days later at 9:00 P.M. came word for Bob Main, MacDonald, Zorthian, and a few others to be down at the airfield by dawn. There was frenzied packing and a great impromptu drinking party with all the old songs of the outfit. Two of those supposed to shove off were down the island and didn't return until 1:00 A.M. One of them was wildly excited. Colonel Roe held up Miller as a witness for a court-martial proceeding. They had left by morning; they had left us; their departure had left a feeling of deep despondency in some of us who were not on the list. The insidious question in my mind was, "Would two months have to intervene before I could make it?"

There were a few small air raids on the island off Motobu. We had built an air strip on Ie Shima. Those nights were a slight departure from monotony.

Then came the 20th of July. Orders! I was on it. So was "Double A" Aadnessen, Honeycutt, Alessandroni, and several others of the old Thirteenth ROC at Quantico. There was a sixteen-hour blur of being paid, of having orders signed, of hurried packing and turning in of combat gear, of a party in Miller's tent of which it is difficult to remember the end after many drinks, many addresses exchanged and songs sung. And, finally, the good-byes, difficult only in the case of those few whom I really liked and would have enjoyed taking along with me.

And, at last, on a Sunday morning, we were in jeeps, waving good-bye to those standing outside the tents. My head was rocky from the liquor of the previous night, but a great delight flooded over me so that I repeated time and again to myself, "Going home; going back safe and sound after almost two and a half years." And I tried to forget about coming out again for that big push to finish Japan.

We reached Yontan, a field now crowded with three thousand or more planes. In the early morning we climbed aboard a C-46,[2] circled our farewell to the costly island, where I suppose I narrowly missed remaining with so many others who never saw this day, and by midafternoon, circled in over our old battery position on Guam to land at Agana Airfield.

Anxious now to fly right on through to San Francisco, we discovered that our travel priorities could not secure further air travel from this crowded transportation hub. So, we sweltered in the heat and in our own impatience at the Casual Battalion camp, scarcely daring to leave the tent for fear we might miss some outgoing means of transport. Temperatures ran in the 100s, and pounds melted away, as did hope of an early, swift return.

Meanwhile, on radio broadcasts came news of that final march of worldwide events. The naval bombardments of the Jap coastline was reported. The Potsdam Conference offered Japan a chance to make peace or take the consequences. (And I felt sure they would take the consequences.) Russia declared war.

At last, we heard there was an escort carrier in the harbor. There was no longer a question of stalling around for plane travel; we were ordered aboard the USS *Card.* Going down to the harbor by truck, I was amazed to see the wonderful network of wide roads and the succession of large warehouses. Being carried by launch to the *Card*'s mooring, I saw the USS *Indianapolis,* the fast cruiser that I had visited in Philadelphia after her shakedown cruise, now heading out to sea and destruction. It was her last time to weigh anchor.[3]

On the *Card,* we were given good bunks with eight to a stateroom, wonderful food—the best I had eaten in two years—sunbathing on the flight deck, fine reading, and a chance for sports. Movies were shown at night on the hanger deck. It was a rest cure. We made a fast cruise past Eniwetok to Pearl Harbor. We learned to our delight that the *Card* would spend three days there and carry us to San Diego. What a break not to have to go to the Casual Camp. We had liberty in Honolulu; we shopped, bought liquor and champagne at the Marine Officers' Club.

Then the bomb was dropped on Hiroshima. I couldn't quite grasp the terrific force of the thing, but the question did arise in our discussions at table, "Could this make the Japs give up?" At the Officers' Club, I bumped into Reichner, who was in Hawaii for naval gunfire school. Hank was somewhat disgruntled about the States after his six months' duty there. He thought the Japs were finished and that they would give in.

We sailed on the final lap, our spirits high. We played all day or read books. "Double A" Aadnessen and I even had pillow fights. The lawyers argued old courts-martial and politics. Paul Burke was in the stateroom, taking good care of a Jap microscope that he had found on Okinawa.

The second A-bomb was dropped when we were a day out from Pearl Harbor. Radio messages of Japan's requests for terms kept us glued to the loudspeakers. On August 13, there was word that we might expect immediate surrender. I stayed up until 2300, but the message failed to come. Then, at 0100 in the morning, Double A woke me, saying that it was definite. I broke out two bottles of champagne, which we finished off together with some whiskey in the stateroom. Then the report was denied. Maybe the whole business was a Jap hoax?

On the 14th of August 1945, we were up early in the carrier's bow, trying to look through the haze for a glimpse of the good old American shore. About midmorning, the sun broke through and, at last, the green-topped, yellow cliffs of the point gleamed their welcome. We ate our last meal, a hasty lunch on the *Card,* the carrier from which, although I did not know it until later, Bob Haas[4] had been catapulted to his death. Radios were announcing that Truman would speak later in the day.

By 1400, we were tied up at the pier receiving the customs men, who didn't look at a thing, and watching the lovely girls of the Navy relief organization preparing fresh milk and doughnuts for us. Midafternoon, the hangar deck crowded, we grasped our luggage. My heart seemed packed tighter than any of the crammed seabags. We filed down the gangplank. A group of people who were clustered around a car radio cheered. I could hear it. Truman was announcing Japan's surrender.

The Second World War was really over; I was home for good. I could see the wharf from which I had sailed twenty-eight months before, but what was the difference? All I wanted was to let Madge know that I was again in the U.S.A. with her, able to celebrate this day of peace and rejoicing.

Appendix A

Command and Staff Roster, Ninth Defense Battalion,
during the New Georgia Campaign, 1943

CO	Lt. Col. William J. Scheyer
Executive Officer	Lt. Col. Wallace O. Thompson (to August 6);
	Lt. Col. Archie E. O'Neil (to August 25);
	Maj. Harold B. Meek
Bn-1	Maj. Benjamin J. Beach
Bn-2	Maj. Harold B. Meek (to August 25);
	Capt. William A. Buckingham
Bn-3	Capt. William C. Givens
Bn-4	Maj. Albert F. Lucas
Tank Platoon Commander	Capt. Robert W. Blake
Demolitions Officer	Marine Gunner Ralph B. Brouse
Medical Officer	Lt. Cdr. (MC) Miles Krepela
Dental Officer	Lt. (MC) Nathan I. Gershon

Seacoast (155 mm Gun) Group

Group Commander	Lt. Col. Archie E. O'Neil (to August 6);
	Maj. Robert C. Hiatt
Executive Officer	Maj. Robert C. Hiatt (to August 6);
	Maj. Frank C. Wenban Jr.
Battery A Commander	Capt. Henry H. Reichner Jr.
Battery B Commander	Capt. Walter Wells

90 mm Antiaircraft Group

Group Commander	Maj. Mark S. Adams (to August 21);
	Maj. Arthur B. Hammond Jr. (to August 28);
	Capt. Norman Pozinsky (to September 3);
	Maj. Arthur B. Hammond Jr.
Executive Officer	Capt. Arthur M. Finkel (to August 21);
	Capt. Norman Pozinsky (August 22–28)
Battery C Commander	Capt. Milton M. Cardwell Jr.
Battery D Commander	Capt. Norman Pozinsky (to August 21);
	Capt. James W. Love
Battery E Commander	Capt. William M. Tracy
Battery F Commander	Capt. Theron A. Smith

Special Weapons Group (Machine Gun and Light AA Group)

Group Commander	Lt. Col. Wright C. Taylor (to September 26);
	Maj. Norman E. Sparling
Executive Officer	Maj. Norman E. Sparling
Battery G Commander	Capt. DeWitt M. Snow
Battery H Commander	Capt. Lynn D. Irvin
Battery I Commander	Maj. Arthur B. Hammond Jr. (to August 21);
	Capt. Mark S. Smith

Source: Maj. Charles D. Melson and Francis E. Chadwick, *The Ninth Marine Defense and AAA Battalions* (Paducah, Ky.: Turner, 1990), 95–100.

Appendix B

Command and Staff Roster, Eleventh Marines,
during the Okinawa Campaign, 1945

CO	Col. Wilburt S. Brown
Executive Officer	Lt. Col. Edson L. Lyman
Bn-3	Maj. Charles D. Harris
H&S Battery	1st Lt. Joseph Ermenc

First Battalion, Eleventh Marines

CO	Lt. Col. Richard W. Wallace
Executive Officer	Lt. Col. George M. Lamon
Bn-3	Maj. Ernest E. Schott
H&S Battery	Capt. Glenn E. Morris
A Battery	Capt. Neal C. Newell
B Battery	Capt. Maurice L. Cater
C Battery	Maj. Lawrence A. Tomlinson Jr.

Second Battalion, Eleventh Marines

CO	Lt. Col. James H. Moffatt Jr.
Executive Officer	Maj. John L. Donnell
Bn-3	Maj. William C. Givens
H&S Battery	1st Lt. Martin R. Bock Jr.
D Battery	Capt. James T. Pearce
E Battery	Capt. Lorenzo G. Cutlip (WIA June 22); Capt. Fritz Stampeli (from June 22)
F Battery	Capt. Robert S. Preston

Third Battalion, Eleventh Marines

CO	Lt. Col. Thomas G. Roe
Executive Officer	Lt. Col. Samuel S. Wooster
Bn-3	Capt. Benjamin H. Brown (to June 6); Maj. Robert E. Collier (from June 7)
H&S Battery	2nd Lt. Charles E. Edwards (WIA April 12); Maj. Everett W. Smith (April 12–26); Capt. Edward T. Haislip (from April 27)
G Battery	Capt. Charles W. Fowler
H Battery	Capt. William R. Miller
I Battery	1st Lt. John L. McDonald Jr. (WIA)

Fourth Battalion, Eleventh Marines

CO	Lt. Col. Leonard F. Chapman Jr.
Executive Officer	Maj. Andre D. Gomez
Bn-3	Capt. James A. Crotinger (to June 12); Maj. Lewis D. Baughman (from June 13)
H&S Battery	Capt. Randall L. Mitchell (to April 30); Capt. Thomas F. Moran (May 1–31); 1st Lt. Gordon C. Petersen (From June 1)
K Battery	Maj. Lewis F. Treleaven (WIA April 28)
L Battery	Capt. Richard M. Moordale
M Battery	Capt. George S. Nixon

Source: www.ibiblio.org/hyperwar/USMC/USMC-M-Okinawa/USMC-M-Okinawa-III.html (accessed July 29, 2009)

Appendix C

U.S. Navy and Marine Corps Phonetic Alphabet, 1943

A	Able		N	Nan
B	Baker		O	Oboe
C	Charlie		P	Peter
D	Dog		Q	Queen
E	Easy		R	Roger
F	Fox		S	Sugar
G	George		T	Tare
H	How		U	Uncle
I	Item		V	Victor
J	Jig		W	William
K	King		X	X-ray
L	Love		Y	Yoke
M	Mike		Z	Zebra

Source: *The Bluejackets' Manual,* 11th ed. (Annapolis, Md.: U.S. Naval Institute, 1943), 842.

Appendix D

Report of FO Duty from April 27 through May 1, 1945—
First Lieutenant Donner, H Battery, Eleventh Marines

Observer was attached to "F" Co., 106th Regt., until 30th of April and to "I" Co., 1st Marines during the remaining twenty-four hours.

All OP's in "F" Co., Z of A were partially masked by ridge lines in the immediate foreground and repeatedly came under heavy enemy artillery, mortar, and rifle fire. Strong resistance and the inability of "F" Co. to advance the front more than 350 yards during the four days limited the choice of more suitable OP.

Targets fired upon were all suspected positions of machine guns and mortars and enemy OP's. Fires generally showed good effect in neutralizing the area, though normal barrages could not be adjusted accurately because of restricted observation to the immediate front. There was repeated evidence reported to FDC that one gun was firing short. Our liaison officer, Capt. Ford, 106th Arty., and this observer noted the delay in obtaining fires through Mayfair and attributed this handicap to the existing system of obtaining clearance for missions.

Nature of enemy resistance: Opposing troops, estimated by the source of their fire and the number of dead, were few in number. They had prepared their defenses on the highest ground, dug in with a net of vertical shafts and horizontal tunnels, from which they emerged to fire Nambus and small mortars at extremely short and effective range. On the afternoon of 28 April, "F" Co. advanced upon a wooded knoll at 7776X2 and was surprised by intensive fire from hidden positions at 25 yards, small mortars firing from the base of shafts. The company suffered about thirty-five casualties and was forced to withdraw. These Jap positions had undergone considerable artillery and mortar preparation for two days.

All Japanese artillery fire appeared to come from positions almost due south, but no gun flash or sound could be observed.

Friendly infantry characteristics: "F" Company displayed a strong will to advance even after the heavy losses of 28 April. They were anxious to use all artillery available and trusted the observer's judgment completely in regards to safety factors. Usually, however, the company was out of touch with units on their flanks, a condition prevailing even at their Bn. CP, where information of the left Bn. of the 106th Regt. was needed. When the company employed tanks, the infantry moved forward aggressively, leading the armor, which was overly cautious. No good teamwork could be obtained because of complete lack of communication with and lack of control of [the] tanks.

"I" Company of the 1st Marines was observed only during the period in which they took over the lines of 2nd Bn., 106th Regt.

Photo coverage of the target areas, even though small in size, as long as they were clear reproductions, would be of inestimable aid to this observer if he could have one to use up forward.

—Christopher S. Donner
1st Lt., USMCR

Notes

Introduction

1. Madge's family had strong literary connections. Col. George C. Haas Sr.'s brother, Robert Haas, was one of the cofounders of Random House, as well as being William Faulkner's agent and publisher and the man principally responsible for bringing Faulkner's works to that publishing house. Madge's father, Colonel Haas, and his brother Bob married two sisters, Clara and Merle. Merle was also well known as being the translator from the French of Laurent de Brunhoff's well-known "Babar the Elephant" children's series published in America by Random House—which books Chris's son "Toph" received as boyhood Christmas presents. E-mail, Dr. Christopher S. Donner III to the editor, February 6, 2010.

2. As Chris Donner III noted, "There was a strong sense of patriotism on my mother's side of the family; all my aunts and my uncle were involved in the war effort, as well as were Robert Haas's children." E-mail, Dr. Christopher S. Donner III to the editor, February 6, 2010. Of Robert and Merle Haas's three children, their son Robert Jr. was a naval aviator whose TBF-1 torpedo plane was lost at sea off the aircraft carrier USS *Card* in May 1943 en route to Casablanca—this same ship would later figure prominently in his brother-in-law Chris's experiences— and a daughter, Elizabeth Haas Pfister, served as a Women's Air Force Service Pilot (WASP), who was finally decorated for her wartime service ferrying Army Air Force aircraft in March 2010. E-mail, Dr. Christopher S. Donner III to the editor, March 14, 2010.

3. Maj. Charles D. Melson and Francis E. Chadwick, *The Ninth Marine Defense and AAA Battalions* (Paducah, Ky.: Turner, 1990), 10.

4. Paul Fussell, *Wartime: Understanding and Behavior in the Second World War* (Oxford, UK: Oxford Univ. Press, 1989), 3–13.

5. A superb overview of these aspects of the Pacific war is provided by the classic study by John W. Dower, *War without Mercy: Race and Power in the Pacific War* (New York: Pantheon, 1986). See also Fussell, *Wartime*, 116–20.

6. See, for example, Bruce I. Gudmundsson, "Okinawa," *MHQ: The Quarterly Journal of Military History* (Spring 1995): 64, 73.

7. While debate still rages among modern historians as to how high the Allied and Japanese casualty lists would have been had Operation Olympic been launched in autumn 1945—and whether estimates of such casualties justified the A-bombings—it is beyond doubt that the Kyushu landings would have been an enormously bloody affair, featuring Japanese "special attack" (i.e., suicide) weapons of all kinds, including women and children armed with bamboo spears; the possible use of poison gas; and hints of contemplation by U.S. planners of using the next available A-bombs as tactical weapons, in a time before the effects of radiation sickness were fully appreciated and understood. See Joseph H. Alexander, *Storm Landings: Epic Amphibious Battles in the Central Pacific* (Annapolis, Md.: Naval Institute Press, 1997), 172–92; George Feifer, *Tennozan: The Battle of Okinawa and the Atomic Bomb* (New York: Ticknor and Fields, 1992), 567–72; Edward J. Drea, "Previews of Hell," *MHQ: The Quarterly Journal of Military History* (Spring 1995): 74–81.

8. It is noteworthy that the enlisted men and other officers of the Ninth Defense's A Battery appreciated their lieutenant, and he certainly made a lasting impression on several of them. As one of Donner's former subordinates, Joe Pratl, noted, "Chris Donner; now, he was a real Marine officer, and he looked the part." A member of the July 2, 1943, burial party overseen by Donner, Pratl recalled Donner's memorial service in the midst of the chaos of Suicide Point, noting that Donner insisted that the men being buried be given a proper service. "We all thought that was a mark of character, and we respected the man for that." Telephone interview with Joseph Pratl, Chicago, Illinois, August 17, 2009. Recalling Donner as a "quiet person [who] did some very heroic things later when a Forward Observer on Okinawa," Chris's A Battery commander, Hank Reichner, recalled in his own memoirs, "Despite our disparate backgrounds, we made a pretty good team and had some quite heated philosophical discussions from time to time." Henry H. Reichner Jr., *But One Life to Give* (New York: Xlibris, 2009), 135.

9. This is a point abundantly noted in numerous other accounts and autobiographies of the war: e.g., see Stephen E. Ambrose, *Band of Brothers: E Company, 506th Regiment, 101st Airborne, From Normandy to Hitler's Eagle's Nest* (New York: Simon and Schuster, 1992), 156 ("Veterans tried to help replacements, but they also took care not to learn their names, as they expected them to be gone shortly. It was not that the old hands had no sympathy for the [replacements]"); Stephen E. Ambrose, *Citizen Soldiers* (New York: Simon and Schuster, 1997), 277–78; Fussell, *Wartime*, 66–67 (citing former marine Eugene Sledge's comments on the perception of replacements on Okinawa: "They were forlorn figures coming up to the meat grinder and going right back out of it like homeless waifs, unknown and faceless to us, like unread books on a shelf").

10. Pratl interview.

11. E. B. Sledge, *With the Old Breed at Peleliu and Tarawa* (Novato, Calif.: Presidio Press, 1981).

12. Melson and Chadwick, *Ninth Marine Defense and AAA Battalions,* 38, 118.

13. Max Hastings, *Retribution: The Battle for Japan, 1944–45* (New York: Ran-

dom House 2008), 374–75, 379, 384; Jack H. McCall Jr., *Pogiebait's War* (New York: Xlibris, 2001), 28, 93–94, 145, 157–58, 173–74, 180, 291, 309, 387–88; Charles D. Melson, *Up the Slot: Marines in the Central Solomons* (Washington, D.C.: United States Marine Corps Historical Center/Government Printing Office, 1993), also available at www.nps.gov/archive/wapa/indepth/extcontent/usmc/pcn-190–003121–00/sec2b.htm (accessed Aug. 12, 2009); Melson and Chadwick, *Ninth Marine Defense and AAA Battalions,* 38, 118.

1. April to June 1943

1. American forces in the Second World War were prohibited from keeping personal diaries and journals. Those who did, such as Marine Eugene B. Sledge, author of *With the Old Breed,* and sailor James F. Fahey, author of *Pacific War Diary, 1942–1945* (Boston: Houghton Mifflin, 1963), hid their notes in Bibles or similar personal effects.

2. The Marines' green service uniform, as opposed to their summer tan uniforms or herringbone-twill field "utilities."

3. A former Matson Lines ocean liner. Regarded as rather luxurious, this liner (built in 1932) had regularly made prewar runs from West Coast ports to Hawaii and Australia.

4. "OC" stands for Officers Candidate Course, and "ROC" stands for Reserve Officers Course. See the glossary for other definitions of other terms and abbreviations that appear throughout this work.

5. "Mothersill's Seasick Remedy" was an early twentieth-century patent medicine often advertised as an antiseasickness and motion-sickness preventative.

6. Equator-crossing ceremonies were a frequent and common occurrence on both military and civilian ships; reminiscent of modern fraternity initiations, these most often involved a visit by King Neptune and his "court," and the administration of various rites of passage and punishments on neophyte "pollywogs" by "shellbacks," those seasoned mariners who had already been initiated into the mysteries of the equator.

7. Part of French Polynesia, New Caledonia's local government had cast its lot with the pro-Allied Free French government in exile.

8. "First MAC" is First Marine Amphibious Corps (also sometimes expressed as "I MAC").

9. Nickname for Australians and New Zealanders (from the acronym for Australian–New Zealand Army Corps).

10. Atabrine was a medicine intended to prevent or lessen malarial symptoms. It was reputed to turn the user's skin yellowish; due to this symptom, and as it was also alleged by some to cause impotence, officers and NCOs often had to take great pains to ensure that their troops took their Atabrine pills.

11. Eight of these weapons—four per Batteries A and B—replaced World War I–vintage, French-designed 155 mm M1917 GPF guns that had earlier comprised the principal armament of the Seacoast Group of the Ninth Defense Battalion on Guadalcanal. Melson and Chadwick, *Ninth Marine Defense and AAA Battalions,* 21.

12. Part of Colonel Scheyer's preinvasion "pep talk" to his Marines went as follows:

What we have done so far will seem small to us a month from now. We have a job which, [if] successfully accomplished, will go down in history. To the men who have been with the battalion from the beginning, I say, "Fine work, men, you have done your job well. I know that you will do the next one." To the new men, I must add a few words of caution. Every unit, including the 9th Defense, when it landed on Guadalcanal, imagined it heard Japs and a good battle started in which our own men were shot. Bear in mind, always, that nighttime is the time for knife-fighting. Do no promiscuous shooting at any time, save your bullets for the Japs. It may be possible that one or two Jap snipers will fire at us from coconut trees, that doesn't mean that every tree has a Jap in it. . . . If any of you have the idea that the Japs are super-men, get it out of your heads. They are fifth raters who have a mistaken notion that they must die for their Emperor and our job is to help them do just that as fast as we possibly can.

Memorandum Order No. 29–43, Headquarters, Ninth Defense Battalion, June 28, 1943, reprinted in Melson and Chadwick, *Ninth Marine Defense and AAA Battalions*, 78. As will be seen in the next chapter, unfortunately not everyone apparently heeded Colonel Scheyer's word of caution on nighttime combat.

2. June 30, 1943, to December 27, 1944

1. Present in Donner's original text, but marked through as a later pen-and-ink deletion, the following appears: "I have never had confirmation of the story of her loss." Serving as the command ship of the New Georgia task force under Rear Adm. Richmond Kelly Turner, the *McCawley* was first hit by Japanese aircraft; then, it was erroneously torpedoed and sunk by a U.S. Navy PT boat that mistook the damaged transport for a Japanese vessel. The facts of this colossal "friendly fire" blunder remained largely unknown until some thirty years after its occurrence. In any event, Donner's recounting of this incident in 1946 and his recognition that the cause was fratricide may tend to undercut allegations that circulated that the true facts were essentially "covered up" by the U.S. Navy until the mid-1970s.

2. The plantation in question was a prewar Lever Brothers coconut palm plantation. Lever Brothers provided one of the largest (if not the largest) commercial ventures in the British Solomon Islands.

3. An International Harvester-made caterpillar tractor, often used as a heavy artillery tractor as well as a bulldozer when fitted with the typical blade attachment.

4. Rain squalls over air bases in the Russells had grounded the American and New Zealand aircrews tasked with providing combat air protection over Rendova, but the storm front left unaffected the Japanese Naval Air Force aerodromes clos-

est to the New Georgia island group. Further contributing to the turn of events that caught the task force flat-footed on July 2, the Ninth's primary long-range search radar was inoperable after its fuel tank had been filled with the wrong kind of fuel. Melson and Chadwick, *Ninth Marine Defense and AAA Battalions*, 25–26; John N. Rentz, *Marines in the Central Solomons* (Washington, D.C.: Headquarters, U.S. Marine Corps/Government Printing Office, 1952), 62–63.

5. In fact, twelve bombers; the thirteenth, a Mitsubishi Zero fighter, was downed by another Ninth Defense Special Weapons Group gun.

6. A very large volcanic island to the west of New Georgia.

7. These Japanese nocturnal raiders were so named because the engines of the twin-motored bombers appeared to be out of synchronization, leading the aircraft to sound like a washing machine. See generally Eric Bergerud, *Touched with Fire: The Land War in the South Pacific* (New York: Viking, 1996), 401.

8. In fact, the first clinical diagnoses of war neurosis, later labeled as "combat fatigue," were identified on New Georgia: 360 soldiers from the Army's Forty-third Division were evacuated for psychological symptoms less than two weeks after the initial landings. This division especially suffered many casualties from friendly troops' attacking one another over supposed "snipers." Chaotic episodes known as "jitterbugging" (after the frenzied 1930s dance craze) or the "jungle jitters"—often involving nighttime friendly fire shootouts—were widely reported in one particular regiment of the Forty-third Division. According to the army's official history of the New Georgia campaign:

> Some men knifed each other. Men threw grenades blindly in the dark. Some of the grenades hit trees, bounced back, and exploded among the Americans. Some soldiers fired round after round to little avail. In the morning no trace remained of Japanese dead or wounded. But there were American casualties: some had been stabbed to death, some wounded by knives. Many suffered grenade fragment wounds, and 50 percent of these were caused by fragments from American grenades. . . . The regiment was to suffer seven hundred [casualties] by July 31.

John J. Miller Jr., *Cartwheel: The Reduction of Rabaul* (Washington, D.C.: Department of the Army, Office of Chief of Military History, 1959), 113. The only immediate correctives for such unit-wide "jitterbugging" incidents were training and adjustment, and the relief of the officers responsible for the men involved in such episodes. After the rash of incidents during the first two weeks of the fighting on New Georgia, incidents of "jitterbugging" ceased to plague the Forty-third almost as mysteriously as they had started. See, e.g., Eric Hammel, *Munda Trail* (New York: Orion, 1989), xiv, 98–100, and 154–57; and Bergerud, *Touched with Fire*, 379–80, 446–52.

9. One of the navy PT boat squadrons based at Tombusolo apparently included the squadron to which Lt. (j.g.) John F. Kennedy's crew and famous boat, *PT-109*, was assigned.

10. On August 1, a Japanese air raid hit the torpedo boat mooring basin at Rendova. Nearby on Tombusolo was Edwin Jakubowski with Ninth Defense Battalion Special Weapons, firing at the attacking aircraft. "A PT Boat was strafed and blew up next to my little island. Plywood flying all over me and one of its torpedoes went by," he recalled. Capt. Theron A. Smith, commanding Battery F, had just inspected his Number 3 Searchlight Section when the attack occurred and later wrote, "some Sunday, alerts and [Condition Reds] all last night and most of the day. Attacked by two dive bombers and Zeros (estimated 50) about 1600. Two PTs destroyed, another sunk and beyond salvage." In a footnote to the campaign, Lt. (jg) John F. Kennedy's *PT 109* was rammed and sunk early the next morning while operating from the Rendova base. Melson, *Up the Slot.*

11. See Melson and Chadwick, *Ninth Marine Defense and AAA Battalions,* 36, 167; Miller, *Cartwheel,* 167, 172; Rentz, *Marines in the Central Solomons,* 123.

12. An example of one of his poems from around this time still exists in the Donner family's files, which contrasted the threats of "Washing Machine Charlie" and the still-frequent Japanese air raids with some of the comforts and joys of civilian life. Dated September 24, 1943, it was titled "You'll Give Your Position Away":

You'll give your position away.
In combat the comforts of life don't pay.
Where once friends beat a path to your door,
That path on an aerial photo in war
Will give your position away.

Civilian gourmets often feel
That picnic fires add zest to a meal.
But shun hot food when you're in the jungle,
A wisp of smoke may be just the bungle
Which will your position reveal.

A line of laundry looks so clean.
Its whiteness casts a purified sheen;
Yet socks and skivvies of snowiest white
Will bring Jap bombers to call on ye:
They let your position be seen.

A moon on high, a night in May,
Her head on your shoulder, a nook of hay.
For soldiers, moons are all out of place:
Bright satellites now are in disgrace,
They give our position away.

Courtesy Dr. Christopher S. Donner III.

13. Navy Mobile Hospital 8, the principal Navy Medical Corps hospital in the sector, a 1,290-bed facility located on Guadalcanal.

14. For more on the liberation and occupation of Guam, see Harry A. Gailey, *The Liberation of Guam* (San Francisco: Presidio Press, 1988); and Cyril J. O'Brien, *Liberation: Marines in the Recapture of Guam; Marines in World War II Commemorative Series* (Washington, D.C.: History and Museums Division, Headquarters, U.S. Marine Corps, 1994); for the Ninth Defense's role, see Melson and Chadwick, *Ninth Marine Defense and AAA Battalions,* 61–74; and for A Battery's experiences in particular, Reichner, *But One Life to Give,* 160–64. According to Col. (ret.) Henry Reichner, the wretched ship on which A Battery found itself for fifty-four days between embarking at Banika and landing on Guam was the *Sea Fiddler,* an army transport with a civilian (likely Merchant Marine) crew; Reichner, *But One Life to Give,* 160.

3. December 27, 1944, to March 31, 1945

1. "Item" being the then-current phonetic usage for the letter "I." See Appendix C for the Navy's and Marines' phonetic alphabet that was used during the Second World War.

2. Landing vehicle tracked (armored) amphibious tractors were first equipped with turret-mounted 37 mm and, by 1945, the LVT (A)-4 with 75 mm guns. These were essentially utilized as amphibious tanks during beach assaults, and 360 of the LVT (A)-4s were to lead another 1,400 unarmored LVTs and 700 DUKW amphibious trucks in a line extending seven miles in the landings on Okinawa. Alexander, *Storm Landings,* 97–99, 155, 167.

3. SCR-510 model FM field radios; principally intended for vehicular usage due to their size and bulkiness.

4. The USS *Franklin* (CV-13) was attacked on March 19, 1945; although ripped apart by Japanese bombs and losing over seven hundred killed, the ship nevertheless did not sink, earning it the nickname "The Ship That Wouldn't Die," and its crew was reputed to be the most decorated crew in U.S. naval history.

4. April 1 to April 12, 1945

1. Consolidated B-24 four-engined heavy bomber.

2. This appears to be a shorthand reference for a standing type of barrage or artillery firing pattern used by the Eleventh Marines.

3. Slang for the SCR-536 handheld radio: also known as a "walkie-talkie" or "handy-talkie," it was the standard Marine rifle company and platoon-level radio set.

4. In a "time burst," each artillery battery fires its shells at a precisely calculated individual time plotted to ensure that every round fired will reach the target area more or less simultaneously; in U.S. Army field artillery parlance, massed time bursts of several batteries firing in this highly coordinated manner were known as "time on target," or "TOT," fires.

5. April 12 to May 6, 1945

1. President Roosevelt died in Warm Springs, Georgia, on April 12, 1945.

2. "Hot spots" indeed; at about this time, one of the most beloved American war correspondents, Ernie Pyle, was killed by Japanese machine-gun fire while accompanying troops of the Army's Seventy-seventh Infantry Division on the small adjoining island of Ie Shima on April 18, 1945.

3. The Japanese 50 mm grenade launcher was known to the Allies as the "knee mortar" because its curved base plate—to the hazard of any Allied soldier who tried firing the weapon in such manner—was mistakenly believed to have been curved to fit the firer's leg or knee. It was not so intended.

4. During this time, Donner also wrote his after-action report for April 27 through May 1, which is reproduced as appendix D. It highlights the agony of Company F's battle for Hill 58, as well as the extent to which the Japanese had honeycombed the area around Hill 58 with caves and tunnels. At the end of this report, Donner politely asks for an aerial photograph of the area he is expected to observe as being "of inestimable aid" to him in his missions; if he ever got such photos from the Battalion's staff, he does not refer to them in the rest of his memoirs.

6. May 7 to June 11, 1945

1. From his description, Donner had just encountered one of the most feared Japanese weapons on Okinawa, the 320 mm "spigot mortar." An extremely simple but powerful weapon, the mortar fired a projectile resembling a finned, flying torpedo that created enormous craters and generated a powerful blast on detonation.

2. This caliber would equate to 120 mm. While the Japanese did use 4.7-inch ex-naval guns in shore installations, it is perhaps likely that the Japanese guns being described by Chris were a pair of the smaller 47 mm Type 1 high-velocity guns frequently encountered by U.S. troops on Okinawa.

3. A type of water purification tablet.

7. June 11 to August 14, 1945

1. On June 18, 1945, Buckner was killed by shrapnel as he and his staff watched an assault by the Eighth Marines. He was one of the two most senior American generals to die in the war—the other being the chief of Army Ground Forces, Lt. Gen. Lesley J. McNair, during Operation Cobra in Normandy in 1944—and the most senior American to be killed by direct enemy fire, McNair having died in a horrendous "friendly fire" airstrike by U.S. Army Air Force bombers.

2. Curtiss "Commando" twin-engined cargo and personnel transport.

3. Torpedoed on July 30, 1945, after delivering A-bomb components to Tinian, the sinking of the heavy cruiser *Indianapolis* by the Japanese submarine *I-58* was the single most deadly loss of life for the U.S. Navy in its history, as only 316 of 1,196 crewmen survived days of exposure, dehydration, and shark attacks. It was also the last major U.S. Navy combat vessel lost in World War II.

4. Robert K. Haas Jr., the only son of Madge Donner's Uncle Bob and Aunt Merle, was a naval aviator and the pilot of a Grumman TBF-1 "Avenger" torpedo bomber that was lost at sea while flying from the *Card* in May 1943, while the carrier was sailing for Casablanca, Morocco.

Glossary

AA: Antiaircraft (sometimes also called "AAA," antiaircraft artillery).

Amphtrack or Amph: See entry for "LVT."

Anzac: Slang for Australia and New Zealand and their inhabitants (from the British World War I designation "ANZAC," Australian–New Zealand Army Corps).

APC: Small coastal transport ship (A = attack transport, P = personnel, C = coastal).

APD: World War I–era, four-stacked Navy destroyer converted to serve as a fast assault transport (A = attack transport, P = personnel, D = destroyer).

Atabrine: Antimalarial compound, reputed to turn the taker's skin a yellowish color.

B-17: Boeing "Flying Fortress" four-engined heavy bomber of the U.S. Army Air Forces.

B-24: Consolidated "Liberator" four-engined heavy bomber of the U.S. Army Air Forces, known as the PB4Y-1 in Navy and Marine Corps service.

BAR: Browning Automatic Rifle M1918, a .30 caliber magazine-fed light machine gun (despite being described as an "automatic rifle").

Base Defense Weapons School: The prerequisite Marine course for young officers scheduled to be assigned to service in Marine Corps defense battalions, where they received training in coast and antiaircraft artillery weapons and tactics.

Battalion-2: Battalion staff-level intelligence officer (other Battalion-level staff officers being the Battalion-1, personnel; Battalion-3, operations; and Battalion-4, logistics and supply).

Boondocking: The state of being "out in the field," "in the boondocks" (a corruption of the Filipino word for a mountainous area, *bundok*), that is, being away from an established camp or post. Marines' field/combat boots were, accordingly, called "boondockers."

C-3: Composition or Compound 3, an early type of U.S. plastic explosive. (Because it burned slowly, it could also be used as a fuel for heating C-ration cans.)

C–46: Curtiss "Commando," twin-engined cargo aircraft; known as the R5C in U.S. Navy and Marine Corps service, it was capable of carrying up to forty troops and had about twice the cargo capacity of the C-47.

C–47: Douglas "Skytrain": twin-engined cargo and transport aircraft, the militarized version of the DC-3 civil airliner, known as the R4D-1 in U.S. Navy and Marine Corps service and capable of carrying up to twenty-seven troops.

Camp Elliott: U.S. Marine Corps camp outside San Diego, named in honor of Maj. Gen. George F. Elliot, the Marine Corps' tenth Commandant (1903–10), and from September 1942, the home of the Fleet Marine Force Training Center, West Coast, and the Second Marine Division.

Cans: Nickname for destroyers (from "tin can," reflecting their light-skinned armor protection).

Cat: See definition of "TD 18" below.

CO: Commanding officer.

Condition Red: Air raid imminent. Its opposite was Condition Green, meaning "all clear."

Corpsman: Navy medical technician, assigned to serve as a medic in a Marine unit.

Corsair: Chance-Vought F4U-1 single-seater fighter of the naval and Marine air wings. Characteristically inverted-gull-winged, with a prominent long nose mounting a powerful radial engine and armed with six .50 caliber machine guns, the versatile Corsair was known by the Japanese as "Whistling Death."

CP: Command post.

C rations: "Ration C," featured a cardboard box containing two cans: one with crackers, powdered coffee or tea, candy, toilet paper, various condiments, and four cigarettes, and the other filled with food to be warmed—among other "menu items," hash, stew, chicken and noodles, and (more frequently than not) the ubiquitous Spam.

Dogface: Near-universal American military nickname for U.S. Army combat troops, particularly infantrymen, for their bearded and grimy faces after days in action.

Dope: News; information.

Exec: Executive officer, the second-in-command of a unit.

F6F: Grumman Hellcat single-seat fighter-bomber, used widely by the U.S. Navy.

FDC: Fire direction center.

FO: Forward observer.

Garand: U.S. .30 caliber M1 semiautomatic rifle.

Greens: Marine service dress uniform, consisting of forest-green colored pants, cap, and coat.

Gunner: Special Marine Corps warrant officer rank for warrant officers serving in a combat capacity; particularly found in Marine artillery units.

Heads: Latrines; toilets.

Headspace: The distance from where the cartridge chamber stops to the face of the bolt face in a weapon; the need to use a special gauge made to check a weapon's headspace before its firing was a particular feature of training for use of .30 and .50 caliber machine guns.

Holy Roller: See definition for "APD."

KIA: Killed in action.

Knee mortar: Japanese Type 89 50 mm grenade launcher; it was fitted with a curved baseplate, which was mistakenly believed by Allied soldiers to be fired from the user's leg. It was not, as many bruised and broken GIs' thigh bones later attested.

K ration: This was issued in three forms, "B," "L," and "D" (the initials should be self-explanatory), Ration K's boxes contained ham and eggs (the usual breakfast entree); canned cheese (the usual lunch selection) or Spam; stew, corned beef hash, or other meat selections; crackers; instant coffee; candy; cigarettes; toilet paper; and gum.

L-5: Stinson "Sentinel" light utility and artillery observation airplane; similar to the Piper Cub, it was also known as the "Flying Jeep" due to its versatility.

LCT: Landing craft, tank.

Liberator: See entry for "B-24."

Long Tom: Nickname for the 155 mm M-1 long-range artillery piece, which equipped both A and B Batteries of the Ninth Defense Battalion's Seacoast (or 155 mm) Group. Firing a 95-pound shell up to 25,395 yards, this very accurate long-barreled gun comprised the heavy armament for defense battalions and many independent Marine heavy artillery units later in World War II.

LSM: Landing ship, medium.

LST: Landing ship, tank.

LVT: Landing vehicle tracked, or "amphtrack"; these amphibious tractors could be personnel/cargo carriers, armored-plated versions—LVT(A)—or armored versions equipped with turret-mounted 37 mm or 75 mm guns, essentially utilized like amphibious tanks.

M-1: Depending on the context, either the .30 caliber M-1 rifle (Garand) or the .30 caliber M-1 carbine.

M-4: American "Sherman" medium tank, usually armed with a 75 mm gun. On Okinawa, some were rearmed with flamethrowers.

M-7: American self-propelled gun, armed with a 105 mm howitzer. Also called the "Priest" due to its pulpit-like cupola next to the gun.

"Mother Sills": Mothersill's patent antiseasickness remedy.

MP: Military Police.

Nambu: Common name of Japanese heavy and light machine guns and Type 14 automatic pistol, so-called for their principal designer, Lt. Gen. Kijiro Nambu.

NCO: Non-commissioned officer (corporals and sergeants).

OC: Marine Officer Candidate School (now called "OCS").
OD: Officer of the day/officer on duty.
OP: Observation point.

PFC: Private, first class.
Pistol Pete: Nickname given to Japanese gun located on Baanga Island that shelled the Munda Point area of New Georgia after its capture by U.S. forces.
PT boat: Patrol torpedo boat.
PX: Post exchange.

QM: Quartermaster.

Replacement Depot: Personnel center that oversaw and temporarily housed replacement troops heading to and from a theater of operations; sometimes referred to by the slang term "repple depple."
ROC: Reserve Officers Course. Equivalent to today's Marine Corps Basic School (TBS), the initial course after OC to teach the former officer candidates the basic skills required of Marine second lieutenants.

SBD: Douglass Dauntless single-engined, two-seater dive bomber.
Seabee: Naval Construction Battalion (C.B.), or one of its members.
Slot, the: See definition for "Tokyo Express."
Spam Can Radio: Marine nickname for the SCR-536 "handy-talkie" or "walkie-talkie" portable radio set.
Special Weapons: Light antiaircraft weapons, in World War II Marine parlance (typically, .50 caliber machine guns and light 20 mm, 37 mm, and 40 mm cannon).

TBF: Grumman "Avenger" single-engined U.S. Navy and Marine Corps torpedo and level bomber, with a three-man crew.
TD 18: International Harvester–manufactured caterpillar tractor ("Cat"), often used as an artillery prime mover in the Ninth Defense Battalion and other U.S. heavy artillery units in the Pacific; also served as a heavy bulldozer. Officially known as the "Tractor, Heavy, M1."
Time on target: A method of coordinating the fires of individual batteries of field artillery to ensure that every projectile fired—no matter the location of the gun firing it—will reach the target area nearly simultaneously.
Tokyo Express: Nickname given to nocturnal Japanese resupply convoys usually led by Japanese rear admiral Raizo Tanaka—typically comprised of destroyers, light cruisers, and transports—off Guadalcanal and in the area of "The Slot," the channel running between the major islands of the Solomons group from Bougainville and the Shortland Islands to Guadalcanal.

WIA: Wounded in action.

WO: Warrant officer.

I MAC: First Marine Amphibious Corps (often pronounced "Eye-Mac").

10-in-1 rations: A prepackaged kind of field ration intended to provide one meal for up to ten men. A typical menu included such canned items as butter-substitute spread, soluble coffee, pudding, meat units, jam, evaporated milk, and vegetables as well as biscuits, cereal, beverages, candy, salt, and sugar. Accessory items were cigarettes, matches, can opener, toilet paper, soap, towels, and water purification tablets.

20 or 20 mm: Light automatic AA gun used by U.S. forces. Capable of firing 450 rounds a minute with a 4,800-yard range, the Swiss-designed 20 mm Oerlikon cannon was roughly similar to a large machine gun and, by mid-1943, was often issued to Marine Corps defense battalions on four-wheeled, automatically operating gun carriages that mounted a pair of these guns as "Twin Twenties."

40 or 40 mm: Bofors 40 mm rapid-fire antiaircraft gun.

47: Japanese 47 mm Type 1 high-velocity gun, originally designed as an antitank weapon.

75: 75 mm artillery piece.

90 or 90 mm: U.S. medium antiaircraft gun of World War II; the M1A1 was originally supplied to Army AA units and was issued to Marine Corps defense battalions beginning in the summer of 1942, the Ninth Defense having twelve of these guns. It had a horizontal range of 18,890 yards and a vertical range of 11,273 yards. It required a full crew of ten men, who, if well trained, could fire twenty-eight rounds per minute.

105: American 105 mm M2 howitzer.

150: Japanese 150 mm gun.

155: A standard bore size of American heavy artillery; these could be either the M1917 GPF or M1 "Long Tom" (see above) long-barreled guns, or the short-barreled M1918 or M1 howitzers.

Index

A Battery ("Able Battery"), Ninth Defense Seacoast Group, 125n11, 129n14; air raids on, 32–33, 36; casualties of, 4–5; damage to guns of, 33, 36; Donner and, 14, 25, 30–31; Donner as Exec of, 25, 42; Donner's reputation in, 15, 124n8; in Guadalcanal campaign, 27, 32–33; moved to Nusalavata, 43–44; on Rendova, 4–5, 31; setting up, 31, 39, 42; strength of, 26, 39; at Tombusolo island, 36–37; Townsend commanding, 44–45
Aadnessen, "Double A," 113, 115
Adelup Point, Guam, Long Tom position above, 44
aerial observation, 93, 102, 130n4
air raids, Japanese: on A Battery, 32–33; on Guadalcanal, 26; on Munda Field, 27, 34, 41; near Ulithi Atoll, 56; on New Georgia campaign, 5, 7; off Motobu, 113; on Okinawa landing beach, 7, 66; on Piru Plantation, 40; planes in, 127n5, 127n6; on PT boats, 128n10; on Rendova beachhead, 5, 30, 32, 35, 36; on Third Battalion camp, 75–76; on Tombusolo island, 37
Alessandroni, 113
American Samoa, 19–20
ammunition: Donner supervising delivery of, 35, 40, 42; handlers for, 39, 103; supply issues with, 32, 75
amphibious tractors (amphtracks), 60,

129n2, 134; artillery practicing with, 49, 51; in landings for Okinawa assault, 52–53, 58–60
antiaircraft (AA) batteries, 30, 37; effectiveness of, 5, 33, 34, 66; Marine defense battalions and, 3–4, 6; Munda Field and, 34, 41
Army, U.S., 31, 33, 46; in assault on Kolombangara, 39, 41–42; assault on Munda by, 35–37; in attack on Wana Ridge, 99–100; FOs supporting, 67–75, 78; landings by, 28, 35; Marines vs., 13, 77–78, 88; in New Georgia campaign, 28, 30, 34, 40–41, 127n8; in Okinawa, 82, 102, 105; planning assaults, 77, 105
artillery. See field artillery
Arundel, New Georgia island group, 39, 41
Asato-gawa, Okinawa river, 103
Atabrine, anti-malaria pills, 24, 26, 125n10, 132
atomic bombs, 9–10, 115, 124n7

B Battery, Ninth Defense Seacoast Group, 39, 41–42, 125n11
Baker, Lt., 21
Ballinger, Warrant Officer Ernest F., 45
Bangarer, Lt. Larry, 22
Banika (Russell Islands), 6, 27, 44
Baron, PFC, A Battery truck driver, 32
Bateman, Lt. Les, 22
Battle of the Bulge, 45–46

media: correspondents in Okinawa, 77–78, 130n2; photographers for, 101

Meek, Maj. Harold B., 24

Melson, Charles D., 15

memoirs, Donner's: changes to, 13, 15–16; motives for writing, 10, 14, 17; OC experiences omitted from, 11; publication of, 15–16; writing of, 1–2, 10; writing style of, 10, 13

memoirs, lack of, 2, 125n1

Merchant Marines, 44

Miami, Donner moving to, 14

Miami Dade Community College, Donner teaching at, 14

Michevich, Lt., 48–49, 79, 105, 109

Midway Islands, Marine defense battalions on, 4

Miller, Capt. William R., 49, 77, 101, 113; FOs and, 67–75, 79

misconduct, Japanese, 8

misconduct, U.S.: against civilians, 8–9, 95, 104; Donner documenting, 7–8

Moffatt, Lt. Col. James H., 48

Monahan, enlisted member of Donner's FO team, 55, 61

morale, 27; effects of Japanese artillery, 96–97; at Okinawa landing, 58

morale, Donner's: loss of friends and, 35, 103, 113; before Okinawa assault, 56–57

mosquitos, on Guadalcanal, 24

"Mother Sill," anti-seasickness pills, 18

Motobu Peninsula, Okinawa, 112–13

Mukue River, Okinawa, 107–9

Munda Field, New Georgia, 4, 41, 43; assault on, 24, 34, 36–39

Munda Point, New Georgia, 4, 39, 41; defensive positions at, 36–37, 42; landing at, 30, 35; preparations for push on, 26–27; supplies at, 30, 42

Nagasaki, atomic bombing of, 115

Naha, Okinawa, 98, 100, 102, 104

naval bases, Marine defense battalions for, 4

Navy, 38, 55, 115, 123n2, 129n13, 130n3; blocking Japanese reinforcements, 35, 95; coast bombardments by, 59, 114; friendly fire by, 102, 108

New Caledonia, 20–22, 125n7

New Georgia island group, 6, 127n8; beauty of, 14, 43; U.S. campaigns in, 4–5, 7, 24, 28, 34. *See also* Munda Point, New Georgia

New Georgia Occupation Force, loss of command vessel of, 4

New Zealand: fighter strip for P-40 fighters of, 41, 126n4; liberty in, 25–26; Ninth Defense promised leave in, 22, 43

Ninth Defense Battalion, Seacoast Artillery Group, 25, 43; Donner assigned to, 3, 22–23; Donner in, 10, 14, 24; on Guadalcanal, 24; histories of, 15; officers of, 42–43; roles in New Georgia campaign, 6, 126n4; split into AA Battalion and Seacoast Group, 45; weapons groups of, 4, 6, 25

Norton, Capt. Kirt W., 49, 54, 65; FO teams with, 58, 61–62; on guerrilla fighters in Okinawa, 63–64; on Okinawa landing, 58–60

Noumea, New Caledonia, 20, 24–25

nurses, 18–19, 23, 112

Nusalavata Island, New Georgia islet, 43–44

Officer Candidate School (OCS), 3; difficulty of, 11–12, 17; Donner's friendships from, 10, 18, 20, 103

officers, Marine, 17, 27, 51; assignments for, 21–22, 50, 79; casualties among, 91–92, 98, 111, 130n1; diversity of, 12; Donner as, 15, 124n8; for Ninth AA Battalion, 45; for Okinawa assault force, 54; personalities of, 12–13, 42, 48; of Seacoast Artillery Group, 25; shuffled around, 49, 79; training of, 11–12

Okinawa: civilians on, 8; Donner leaving, 114; Donner's anxiousness to leave, 103–4

Okinawa campaign, 8, 124n9; Army and Marines in, 13, 78; bombardment for, 57; casualties in, 9–10, 111; Donner's forward observer team on, 2, 7, 62; Donner's morale before, 56–57; expectations of resistance to, 55, 57; guerrilla fighters in, 63–64; Japanese resistance in, 59–60, 63–65; Japanese withdrawal from, 61, 66; in Japan's Home Islands' defensive shield, 6; landing for, 55, 58–60; organizing advance in, 65; practice landings for,